LOVE OR DIE

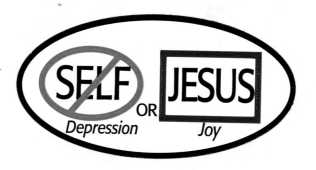

Other books by Alexander Strauch include:

Biblical Eldership:
An Urgent Call to Restore Biblical Church Leadership

The Study Guide to Biblical Eldership:
Twelve Lessons for Mentoring Men for Eldership

Meetings That Work

The New Testament Deacon: Minister of Mercy

The Hospitality Commands

Agape Leadership:
Lessons in Spiritual Leadership from the Life of R.C. Chapman
(coauthored with Robert L. Peterson)

Men and Women: Equal Yet Different

A Christian Leader's Guide to Leading With Love

LOVE OR DIE

Christ's Wake-Up Call to the Church
Revelation 2:4

Alexander Strauch

Lewis & Roth Publishers

Love or Die

ISBN-10: 0-93608-328-X

ISBN-13: 978-0-93608-328-5

Copyright © 2008 by Alexander Strauch. All rights reserved.

Editor: Amanda Sorenson and Shannon Wingrove

Cover Design: Eric Anderson (www.resolutiondesign.com)

Printed in the United States of America

Second Printing 2009

Library of Congress Control Number: 2008933524

To receive a free catalog of books published by Lewis and Roth Publishers, please call toll free 800-477-3239 or visit our website, *www.lewisandroth.org*. If you are calling from outside the United States, please call 719-494-1800.

Lewis and Roth Publishers

P.O. Box 469

Littleton, Colorado 80160

Contents

Introduction

Pursue love....
1 Cor. 14:1

My first encounter with the biblical principles of love started in a negative way during my early years as a born-again Christian. I was surprised when I saw true believers fight, display angry attitudes, and separate from one another. To make matters worse, the conflicts I witnessed weren't about lofty, eternal theological issues of the gospel, but rather, personal preferences and church traditions. To me, as a young believer, fighting among older, godly believers was quite discouraging.

To deal with my disillusionment, I began to search the New Testament for answers as to what should really be important in the life of the local church. What are correct Christian priorities and attitudes? How can true believers disagree without mutual destruction (Gal. 5:15)? What I discovered, among other things, was what I called, at the time, the moral (or Christlike) character of the church. The church is to be a family of brothers and sisters characterized by humility, gentleness, peace, forgiveness, forbearance, faith, hope, and love, with love being the supreme, overarching virtue. "And above all these," writes Paul, "put on love, which binds everything together in perfect harmony" (Col. 3:14).

First Corinthians 13, in particular, spoke to me about the fact that there is a "more excellent way" of thinking and behaving, and that the greatest theological knowledge, the most extraordinary spiritual gifts, and most sacrificial services are profitless—even hurtful—if not motivated and colored by the spirit of Christlike love. As a result of my Bible study, I realized the priority of love in all that we do and say.

My next life-changing encounter with Christian love came several years later when a friend gave me a biography of Robert Cleaver Chapman. R. C.

1

Chapman was known for living a life of love without compromising the truths of Scripture. His life of love has been an inspiration and challenge to many of God's people. His biography confirmed in my mind what I had already seen in my study of Scripture: Love is essential to everything we do in Christian life and ministry.

My third memorable encounter with love came while studying the Book of Ephesians and using the acclaimed commentaries of D. Martyn Lloyd-Jones, once preacher at Westminster Chapel in London. As I studied Ephesians 3:18-19, I experienced a life-changing realization of the love of Christ for me. Paul's prayer that we might know intellectually, personally, and experientially the immeasurable love of Christ for his people had a powerful impact on me:

> I bow my knees before the Father…that…he may grant you to be strengthened with power through his Spirit in your inner being,… that you…may have strength to comprehend with all the saints what is the breadth and length and height and depth [of Christ's love], and to know the love of Christ that surpasses knowledge. (Eph. 3:14-19)

As a result of these encounters, I developed a life-long interest in the subject of biblical love; I have subsequently written several books on love, *particularly as it applies to developing loving church leadership and a loving church community*. (See Appendix A for a list of these books on love.) Although my interest in this thrilling subject continues to grow, I always feel a terrible sense of inadequacy in trying to write about Christlike love. Unlike writing about other biblical subjects, writing about love constantly exposes one to his or her failures to love God and neighbor as a Christian should. It is a very convicting subject that touches every aspect of life. I pray that my efforts awaken Christians to the need for our personal lives and our local churches to be marked by the love of Jesus Christ.

Part One

The Problem of Lost Love

You have abandoned the love you had at first.
Rev. 2:4

By means of satellite imagery and software programs that can find almost any address on the planet, I can see almost any church building in the world from my study at home. If, for example, I want to see a certain church in South Africa, I can open a software application and a spectacular picture of our blue and green planet spinning in space appears on my computer screen. I type in *Africa* and the spinning planet rotates to the giant continent of Africa. I then type in *South Africa* and zoom in on the country of South Africa. I type in *Barberton* (a city west of Swaziland), and in seconds I see the entire city. Finally, I type in the address of the church. Before I know it, I'm looking down at the roof of a church building 9,800 miles (15,680 km) from my home.

As powerful and amazing as this technology is, however, I still can't see inside the building. I see only the roof. I cannot see or hear God's people as they worship, nor can I look into the hearts and minds of the people who gather there. But there is one who can see perfectly into every human heart. He can perceive the corporate spirit of a church. Not only can he see into every church and every heart, he can walk among the churches on earth without being detected! And he does it all without the benefit of our feeble computers, cameras, or satellite imagery.

In fact, Christ has been walking among the churches for almost two thousand years. Near the end of the first century, Jesus Christ peered into seven specific churches. He did not just look down at rooftops. He examined the corporate spirit of the church and probed the mind and heart of each believer. Then, in the last book of the Bible, the Revelation to John, Christ reveals his evaluation of each of these seven churches.

Imagine if Christ were to look down at your church, walk in your midst, and give you his evaluation. It would be unnerving to say the least! But in a sense, Christ has already done this. Through the letters to the seven churches of Asia Minor (modern-day Turkey), he addresses the problems and victories, strengths and weaknesses that are common to local churches today.

Too often we care more about church-growth strategies or the latest trends than we do about what Jesus Christ thinks.

Therefore, Christ's evaluation of these seven churches should be of paramount concern to us. His evaluation is perfect. He cannot be deceived. He has eyes "like a flame of fire" (Rev. 1:14) that penetrate the deepest recesses of the heart. All things are open to his scrutiny. Without his evaluation, we are easily deceived and blinded to our errors. Too often we care more about church-growth strategies or the latest trends than we do about what Jesus Christ thinks. But as John Stott reminds us, Christ's evaluation of a church is what ultimately matters. Christ alone "is the church's founder, head, and judge."[1]

We can learn much from Christ's evaluation of each of the seven churches of Asia Minor, but we will focus this study on his evaluation of the church in Ephesus. It addresses the issue of love, particularly the problem of love that has grown cold. This issue is of utmost importance because love is vital to the survival of our local churches today. The text of Christ's evaluation is found in Revelation 2:1-6:

> To the angel of the church in Ephesus write: "The words of him who holds the seven stars in his right hand, who walks among the seven golden lampstands.
>
> 'I know your works, your toil and your patient endurance, and how you cannot bear with those who are evil, but have tested those who call themselves apostles and are not, and found them to be false. I know you are enduring patiently and bearing up for my name's sake, and you have not grown weary. But I have this against

---

[1] John R. W. Stott, *What Christ Thinks of the Church: An Exposition of Revelation 1-3* (Grand Rapids: Baker, 2003), 7.

you, that you have abandoned the love you had at first. Remember therefore from where you have fallen; repent, and do the works you did at first. If not, I will come to you and remove your lampstand from its place, unless you repent. Yet this you have: you hate the works of the Nicolaitans, which I also hate.'"

Chapter One

Christ's Commendation and Complaint

It wasn't easy being Christ's lampstand in a dark, pagan city like Ephesus. Expositor R. H. Charles comments that "Ephesus was...a hotbed of every kind of cult and superstition."[2] The pagan temple of Artemis (Roman Diana) dominated the city and was considered one of the seven wonders of the ancient world. Emperor worship (the imperial cult) thrived in Ephesus and was a required duty of every citizen. Moreover, the city was a prosperous trade center and an immoral port city.

Knowing all this, the Lord graciously acknowledges their "toil" and "patient endurance." He praises this church because it had no tolerance for those who profess the Christian faith but justify an immoral lifestyle: "I know.... You cannot bear with those who are evil." Jesus also praises them for testing "those who call themselves apostles and are not." Like the Berean believers, the Ephesians examined "the Scriptures daily to see if these things were so" (Acts 17:11). When self-proclaimed apostles came to teach, the church tested their claims of apostolic authority and found them to be false. Consequently, the church found the teachers to be self-deceived agents of Satan—not representatives of Christ—and rejected them and their teaching. You can be sure this took courage and determination.

We know, then, that the church at Ephesus was a doctrinally discerning church. It loved truth and hated, as did Jesus, "the works of the Nicolaitans," an immoral, heretical Christian sect (Rev. 2:6). Please take note: Jesus commends them for hating the corrupt teachings and practices of this false sect.

---

[2] R. H. Charles, *The Revelation of St. John*, ICC (New York: Scribner, 1920), 1: 48.

Their hatred of the works of darkness was a demonstration of their love for Christ and God's Word. Churches today need to understand that hatred of evil and falsehood is not a contradiction of love, but an essential part of genuine Christian love (1 Cor. 13:6). Love abhors "what is evil" and clings "to what is good" (Rom. 12:9). The Ephesian believers, then, were role models of theological vigilance. They were defenders of the truth and lovers of the gospel. They were uncompromising in their stand for biblical principles, and for this our Lord highly praises them.

There was much to commend the church in Ephesus, and we should prize all of its exemplary qualities.

We also know that the Ephesians had faced great conflict. They had resisted the agents of Satan and patiently endured many other trying circumstances. So the Lord praises them, saying, "You are enduring patiently and bearing up for my name's sake and you have not grown weary." What a display of their loyalty and dedication!

There was much to commend the church in Ephesus, and we should prize all of its exemplary qualities. The church could have written a best-selling manual on successful church ministry. However, all was not well. Something was fundamentally wrong, and Jesus Christ puts his finger right on the problem: Loss of love. In light of all the commendable qualities of this church, we might think of Christ's complaint as trivial, but in his eyes, the church had "fallen." It had abandoned the love it once had. To the one "who loves us and has freed us from our sins by his blood" (Rev. 1:5), this is no small matter. Thus our Lord says, "I have this against you."

A Failure of Love

Our Lord's complaint against the church at Ephesus is "you have abandoned the love you had at first." Literally translated, the text reads: "You have abandoned your love, the first." Emphasis is placed on the adjective *first*, so the love they abandoned refers to their love as it was first expressed at the beginning of their life together as a church body.

Jesus doesn't say, "You have no love." He says, "You have abandoned the love you had at first." Their love was not what it used to be. While they still had some measure of love because they were, for the most part, true Christians and enduring hardship for his "name's sake" (Rev. 2:3), they no longer possessed the kind of love they had in their early years as a church. They still loved the Lord, but not like they did at first. They still loved one another, but not like before.

Their love for Christ and for one another had once motivated all they did. It brought joy, creativity, freshness, spontaneity, and energy to their life and work. But now their energy source was depleted. Their work had become mundane, mechanical, and routine, and their lives the picture of self-satisfaction. Instead of their love abounding, it had been lacking. Instead of being motivated by love from the heart, their works had become perfunctory. Even certain "works," which sprang from their former love, vanished. For this, Jesus rebukes them and calls them to do those works again (Rev. 2:5).

The object of their lost love is not stated. The text does not say love for Christ or love for fellow believers. It is best, then, to understand Jesus to mean Christian love in general, which would include love for God, love for one another in the church, and love for the lost. According to our Lord, love for God and neighbor are inseparable companions (Mark 12:29-31; Luke 10:27). It is impossible to love God and not love his people or to love his people and not love God (1 John 4:7-5:3).

Jesus uses strong words in his complaint against the Ephesians. Jesus squarely places the responsibility at their feet when he says, "you have abandoned" or "given up"[3] the love they once had. They can't blame anyone else for this loss. They have had every advantage provided by years of good teaching, access to almost all of the New Testament Scriptures, and the power of the indwelling Holy Spirit. No wonder Christ expresses extreme displeasure with the situation in Ephesus. Their loss of love is their fault. They have failed to "keep" themselves in the love of God (Jude 21). They must now face this fact and respond to Christ's criticism and counsel.

---

[3] *BDAG*, s.v., *"aphiēmi,"* 156.

1-5 ohn into

Ephesus - (paul)

Ephesians 5 1-2

Mathew 22 36-40

Chapter Two

When a Church Loses Its Love

Every local church has its own personality, identity, distinctives, gifts, and atmosphere. These differences can be observed in the various churches of the New Testament (Acts 17:11). The one quality, however, that should beautify every believer and every church, regardless of giftedness or personality, is love. Thus the thing that should be of utmost concern to every believer and every church is this: Does a Christlike spirit of love permeate the atmosphere of our church?

The church in Ephesus was not a new church. It was a well-established church sound in doctrine and faith. The Ephesian believers, you can be sure, attended church regularly, knew their doctrine, celebrated the Lord's Supper, rejected false teachers, did good deeds, carried out their responsibilities, lived upright lives, prayed, and sang, but they lacked love.

> *The one quality, however, that should beautify every believer and every church, regardless of giftedness or personality, is love.*

D. A. Carson, professor at Trinity Evangelical Divinity School, wrote an article on Revelation 2:4 titled *A Church that Does All the Right Things, But....*

Describing this kind of church, Carson writes:

> They still proclaim the truth, but no longer passionately love him who is the truth. They still perform good deeds, but no longer out of love, brotherhood, and compassion. They preserve the truth and witness courageously, but forget that love is the great witness to truth. It is not so much that their genuine virtues have squeezed love out, but that no amount of good works, wisdom, and discernment in matters of church discipline, patient endurance in hardship,

hatred of sin, or disciplined doctrine, can ever make up for love-lessness.[4]

Let me illustrate what the kind of lovelessness that so deeply offends our Lord looks like. A popular young preacher and Bible teacher visited a church to preach. He was a good teacher and you could sense his love for the Word and for people. During a time of prayer with a few believers prior to the service, he joined them, asking for God's Spirit to speak to the people, especially the unconverted. After the service, he stood at the front door greeting each individual. It was obvious that he enjoyed talking to the people. In fact, he was the last person to leave the church. He then went to the home of the family he was staying with and had dinner with other people from the church. It was a delightful time of fun, fellowship, and profitable conversations.

Fifteen years later, the same preacher returned to the church to speak. He still preached the Word faithfully, defended sound doctrine, studied hard, kept a busy schedule, and greeted everyone in a friendly manner, but something was different. During the time of prayer before the service, he kept silent. After preaching, he rushed to the front door, but displayed only superficial pleasantries with those he greeted. Within fifteen minutes, he left the church. He no longer shared a meal with people from the church, and he insisted on staying in a hotel rather than in someone's home.

Something had changed in this preacher's life and ministry. While there is nothing necessarily wrong with wanting to stay at a hotel or stipulating an honorarium, in this case these were subtle indicators of a change in spirit. He didn't pray when others did. He didn't spend time with brothers and sisters as he once did. He left the church as soon as possible. Even his preaching seemed more scripted than heartfelt. Many who heard him may not have sensed the change, but some did. What was the difference? He had lost the love he had previously displayed. Jesus would say to this preacher, "I have this against you, that you have abandoned the love you had at first."

Why Is Love So Important?

Why is the loss of love so serious? Why does it distress our Lord so deeply? Why is his threat of judgment so severe? Why is it a life or death issue for a

---

[4] D. A. Carson, "A Church that Does All the Right Things, But…," *Christianity Today* (June 29, 1979): 30.

Matt 22:3̶5̶-40

local church? The answers are provided by Christ himself and those he commissioned as apostles.

First, Jesus taught that "the great and first commandment" is to love God completely, totally, and unreservedly—with *all* one's heart, with *all* one's soul, and with *all* one's mind (Matt. 22:37-38; Mark 12:28-34). The sum of all God's commandments and all religious service is love for God. It is the believer's first priority. It is the reason we were created. Nothing in life is more right, more fulfilling, and more rewarding than loving God our Creator and Savior.

Second, Jesus declared the second commandment is like the first: "You shall love your neighbor as yourself" (Matt. 22:39). Jesus makes love for God and neighbor inseparable companions. He summarized the heart of genuine religion, true inner spirituality, and all moral conduct by the double command to love God and love your neighbor. His own assessment of love is: "On these two commandments depend all the Law and the Prophets" (Matt. 22:40), and "There is no other commandment greater than these" (Mark 12:31).

Hence, Christ's followers are to be *marked not only by total devotion to God but also by sacrificial service to neighbor.* This neighbor love, according to Jesus, includes loving our enemies, our persecutors, and the unlovely (Matt. 5:43-48). Before you read any further, be sure you have grasped the importance of these two commandments for living the Christian life. *John 13:14)*

Third, true discipleship requires denying self and loving him above all others: "Whoever loves father or mother more than me is not worthy of me, and whoever loves son or daughter more than me is not worthy of me. And whoever does not take his cross and follow me is not worthy of me" (Matt. 10:37-38). All other relationships, even the closest family ties, become idolatrous when Christ is not loved first and foremost. *John 13:34-35*

Fourth, Jesus left his followers a new commandment: "A new commandment I give to you, that you love one another: just as I have loved you…. By this all people will know that you are my disciples" (John 13:34). Jesus points to his own example of self-sacrificing love as the pattern for keeping the new commandment. In addition, he taught that it would be by this kind of self-giving love for one another that the world would identify his followers. Indeed, love "is to be the distinguishing mark of Christ's followers." [5]

No ancient or modern philosopher—Plato, Aristotle, Kant, Russell—ever

---

[5] Leon Morris, *The Gospel According to John,* NICNT (Grand Rapids: Eerdmans, 1995), 562.

And one of the scribes...asked him,
"Which commandment is the most important of all?"
Jesus answered, "The most important is,
'Hear, O Israel: The Lord our God, the Lord is one.
And you shall love the Lord your God with all your heart
and with all your soul and with all your mind
and with all your strength.'
The second is this: 'You shall love your neighbor as yourself.' There is
no other commandment greater than these."
And the scribe said to him, "You are right, Teacher.
You have truly said that he is one,
and there is no other besides him.
And to love him with all the heart
and with all the understanding and with all the strength,
and to love one's neighbor as oneself, is
much more than all whole burnt offerings and sacrifices."
And when Jesus saw that he answered wisely, he said to him, "You are
not far from the kingdom of God."

(Mark 12:28-34)

Sets Christians Apart

taught such far-reaching ideas about love. No political figure, from Julius Caesar to Winston Churchill, has made such demands upon his followers to love. And no religious teacher, whether Buddha, Confucius, or Mohammed, ever commanded his followers to love one another as he loved them and gave his life for them. No other system of theology or philosophy says so much about the divine motivation of love (and holiness), or expresses love to the degree of Christ's death on the cross, or makes the demands of love like the teaching of Jesus Christ and his apostles.

"The new commandment," writes Carl Hoch, "is the *sine qua non* of the Christian life."[6] *Sine qua non* (SIH-neh kwah nohn) is a Latin phrase meaning "without which nothing." Thus the new commandment is an essential element of the Christian life and witness to the world. To neglect the new commandment would render the Christian life as "nothing"—as not Christian. In the words of the Scottish New Testament scholar John Eadie, "There is nothing so remote from Christ's example as a hard and uncharitable disposition."[7]

> *"All love is but a reflection or shadow of intratrinitarian love."*
> —KELLY KAPIC

Fifth, John, the beloved disciple of Christ, declared that "God is love" (1 John 4:8, 16). To better understand this statement, we need to look at the Trinity. At the heart of the Christian doctrine of love is the triune nature of God.[8] The ultimate model of love exists among the three Persons comprising the Godhead – God the Father, God the Son, and God the Holy Spirit – who are three in one and one in three and perfect in mutual love. "All love," asserts Kelly Kapic, "is but a reflection or shadow of intratrinitarian love."[9] There has eternally existed a dynamic social relationship between Father, Son,

---

[6] Carl B. Hoch, Jr., *All Things New: The Significance of Newness for Biblical Theology* (Grand Rapids: Baker, 1995), 145.

[7] John Eadie, *Divine Love: A Series of Doctrinal, Practical and Experimental Discourses* (1856; Birmingham, AL: Solid Ground Christian Books, 2005), 276.

[8] "Christianity, in the last analysis, is Trinitarianism. Take out of the New Testament the person of the Father, the Son, and the Holy Spirit, and there is no God left" (William G. T. Shedd, "Introductory Essay" in Philip Schaff, ed., *Nicene and Post-Nicene Fathers,* First Series [1887; Peabody, MA: Hendrickson, 1994], 3: 10-11).

[9] Kelly M. Kapic, *Communion With God: The Divine and the Human in the Theology of John Owen* (Grand Rapids: Baker, 2007), 231.

and Holy Spirit characterized by love (John 17:24).[10] And we have been called
to share in this holy community of love (John 17:26;14:21;15:9-10).

John's magisterial proclamation that "God is love" actually supports his
main appeal to love one another: "Love is from God, and whoever loves has
been born of God and knows God. Anyone who does not love does not know
God, because God is love" (1 John 4:7-8). So not to love one another in the
family of God is an egregious sin.

Sixth, Paul called love the "more excellent way" of living. Love is the chief
virtue that should govern all we do and say in the Christian life. To drive home
this rock-bottom, foundational truth with unforgettable force, Paul writes

> And I will show you a still more excellent way. If I speak in the
> tongues of men and of angels, but have not love, I am a noisy gong
> or a clanging cymbal. And if I have prophetic powers, and under-
> stand all mysteries and all knowledge, and if I have all faith, so as
> to remove mountains, but have not love, I am nothing. If I give
> away all I have, and if I deliver up my body to be burned, but have
> not love, I gain nothing. (1 Cor. 12:31-13:3)

In paraphrase form, Paul is saying:
• Without love, even heavenly tongues sound annoying
• Without love, knowing it all theologically and philosophically helps
  no one
• Without love, powerful, risk-taking faith is worthless
• Without love, giving everything to the poor is unprofitable
• Without love, even the ultimate sacrifice of one's life is pointless

---

[10] Speaking of the Trinity as a "society of Persons," Bruce Ware writes: "God is never
"alone."... The one God is three! He is by very nature both a unity of Being while also
existing eternally as a society of Persons.... He is a socially related being within himself. In this tri-Personal relationship the three Persons love one another, support one
another, assist one another, team with one another, honor one another, communicate
with one another, and in everything respect and enjoy one another.... Such is the rich-
ness and the fullness and the completion of the social relationship that exists in the
Trinity" (Bruce A. Ware, *Father, Son, and Holy Spirit: Relationship, Roles & Relevance*
[Wheaton: Crossway, 2005], 20-21).

Maurice Roberts, Scottish pastor and former editor of *The Banner of Truth*, captures the intense seriousness of Paul's words when he writes,

> In these familiar words we possess one of the most central principles of the Christian faith. It is this. No religious act is of any value in God's sight if it does not accompany and flow from Christian love....
>
> But men seldom ponder it seriously. If the implications of this one principle were consistently thought through, they would have a momentous effect upon us all....
>
> Since nothing is of value in God's eye if it does not flow from love, then how much need there is for us all to correct our habitual formalism!
>
> The problem of formalism, nominalism or religious "coldness" is intensely serious, for the obvious reason that it springs from absence of love to God.... God takes special notice of the way and manner in which men think of him as they attend to his service and worship.[11]

Paul sums up 1 Corinthians 13, the great love chapter, with this statement: "faith, hope, and love abide, these three; but the greatest of these is love." Every Christian is to be marked by faith, hope, and love. These cardinal virtues are foundational to a regenerated life as well as to a thriving local church. Yet even among these three, Paul says, "the greatest of these is love." So whether we are speaking of the fruit of the Spirit or of cardinal virtues, love is the greatest![12]

So whether we are speaking of the fruit of the Spirit or of cardinal virtues, love is the greatest!

---

11 Maurice Roberts, "The Supreme Grace of Christian Love," *The Banner of Truth*, (February, 1989): 1, 3.

12 French pastor and expositor Gaston Deluz summarizes 1 Corinthians 13 in this way: "The vitality of a church, then, is measured by the wealth of its love, not by the fanaticism of its members, the subtlety of its theology or the prosperity of its finances. But it is true that love may increase the zeal of the parishioners, inspire the theologians and improve the finances of the Church" (Gaston Deluz, *A Companion to 1 Corinthians* [London: Darton, Longman & Todd, 1963], 188).

So we must ask, when people visit your church, do they find a warm, friendly, and welcoming atmosphere that demonstrates love for all people? Do they sense Christlike compassion and the kind of loving family community envisioned by the New Testament writers? Do they see genuine care for one another's needs, Christian hospitality, and unselfish generosity? Do they observe joy in the Lord, spiritual vitality, and people reaching out to minister to a suffering world?

Or does your church seem more like an impersonal gathering of people than a spiritual family? Do visitors sense unfriendliness and indifference? Do they see a proud, critical spirit, or an angry, contentious group of people?

Remember, there is always one who walks among the churches, unseen but seeing all. How do you imagine Christ might evaluate your local church body?

A friend of mine had to find a new church after his church had closed. He lived in a large city with many evangelical churches, so he had a wide variety of churches to choose from. He's the kind of person who gets involved and sticks faithfully with his church family, so he wasn't going to settle for just any church. After a long and frustrating search, he finally found a new church family.

I asked him what he had learned from visiting many different churches. He had a number of interesting observations, but I was most interested in why he decided on the church he chose. He said his decision was based on "the spirit of the church, its atmosphere." All the churches he visited were doctrinally sound churches and some were excellent Bible teaching churches; however, something was missing. The church he chose had both good Bible teaching plus a loving, caring spirit among the people. In other words, he had found a loving church family of which he could be a part.

The church in Ephesus was sound in doctrine and faithful to the gospel, but something was missing. The spirit of the church was defective. It lacked love. So let us explore Christ's remedy for its lack of love so we can guard against such a failure in our own churches.

Chapter Three

Christ's Remedy

What we learn from Revelation 2:4, and must never forget, is that an individual or a church can teach sound doctrine, be faithful to the gospel, be morally upright, and work hard, yet be lacking love and therefore, be displeasing to Christ. Love can grow cold while outward religious performance still appears to be acceptable—or even praiseworthy.

We have a tendency to trust in external religious rituals, traditions, denominational distinctions, doctrinal correctness, and moralistic rules, while we overlook the essential, foundational elements of love for God and neighbor. How easy it is to be self-

> *Love can grow cold while outward religious performance still appears to be acceptable—or even praiseworthy.*

satisfied with external religious performance and be like the Pharisees who "tithe mint and rue and every herb, and neglect justice and the love of God" (Luke 11:42).[13] External religious performance can insidiously replace true, inner faith and heartfelt love. This is an ever-present danger. It is a problem that is often difficult to identify or explain until it is too late. Yet it must be identified and corrected because love for God and neighbor lies at the very heart of genuine spiritual life. Thus, Revelation 2:4 is a wake-up call to all churches: love or die!

It is not easy, however, to restore a heart that is deficient in love. There is a physical heart condition called cardiomyopathy that weakens the heart muscle so that the heart can no longer sufficiently pump blood. If left untreated, such

---

[13] For an example of one scribe who understood the foundational truth of love for God and neighbor underpinning all external "burnt offerings and sacrifices," see Mark 12:33-34.

a condition will cause a person to become weaker and weaker and eventually die. There is a similar risk when a heart has become deficient in love. A cold heart becomes a hard heart, a heart that is resistant to change. As time passes, it becomes increasingly difficult to restore the warmth of Christian love. The progression must be stopped and the situation reversed before it's too late.

In the church at Ephesus, a spiritual heart disease, *love deficiency,* was weakening the church. If the condition was not diagnosed and properly treated, the church would die. Instead of growing stronger in love, as a healthy church should, the church was becoming weaker. The Great Physician put his finger on the problem, diagnosed the condition, and prescribed the remedy.

Calling the Ephesians to action, Jesus ominously warned, "I will come to you and remove your lampstand from its place, unless you repent" (v. 5). If they didn't act, he would. This was no idle threat, and it demonstrates how strongly Christ feels about forsaking first love.

Although the exact meaning of Christ's pronouncement is debated, the seriousness of the situation is clear. His words reveal the Ephesians' sick spiritual condition. Lack of love is a life-threatening disease, one they had brought on themselves by their own neglect. If they did not repent, Jesus Christ would remove their light.

To help the church's weakening spiritual heart condition, Jesus directs his people to do three things to avoid divine discipline. Their situation is not beyond repair, but failure to act quickly would mean disaster for the church. So Jesus prescribed a three-fold remedy: remember, repent, and do the deeds they did at first.

Remember

The first thing the Lord directs the church to do is, "Remember therefore from where you have fallen." Jesus says they have fallen; they have backslidden; they are not what they once were spiritually.

Ironically, the church was not deceived by false teachers from without (v. 2), but was deceived by the failure of love within. The Ephesians successfully confronted one grave danger—false teaching—but had succumbed to another equally deadly danger—lack of love. This is a lesson to all churches: Sound doctrine and fervent love both must be maintained and balanced.

To help the Ephesians recognize the seriousness of their condition, Jesus admonished them to remember their early days when love motivated all that they did. They needed to recall the love they originally possessed but had forsaken.

To "remember" means to recollect past feelings and actions, but not in a passive sense. It is not sentimental daydreaming about the "good old days" with no intention to act. The present imperative command, "remember," emphasizes an ongoing, continuous mental attitude of remembering. It requires making the effort to recall past joys, deeds, attitudes, and experiences in the life of the church in order to repeat them and act upon them.

These memories will guide the church's present action and provide future direction. They will set the standard and will motivate change. Remembering these things will help the church see and admit its lapse of love. Remembering will lead to repenting and returning to the first acts of love. For this church, the way forward is by going back: clearly identifying what they had lost and acknowledging their fallen, sinful condition.

Repent

The imperative command "remember" is followed by another imperative command "repent." They must sense the need to return and restore the love they once possessed. Remembering from where they had fallen would lead them to repentance.

What is repentance? D. A. Carson gives a good definition of *repentance:*

> What is meant is not a merely intellectual change of mind or mere grief, still less doing penance, but a radical transformation of the entire person, a fundamental turnaround involving mind and action and including overtones of grief, which results in "fruit in keeping with repentance." Of course, all this assumes that man's actions are fundamentally off course and need radical change.[14]

Through repentance, the church in Ephesus would demonstrate
* that it *accepts* Christ's evaluation of its fallen condition,
* that it has *judged itself* according to Christ's Word to be sinful and deserving of divine discipline (1 Cor. 11:31-32),

---

[14] D. A. Carson, *Matthew 1–12,* The Expositor's Bible Commentary (Grand Rapids: Zondervan, 1995), 99.

- that it *grieves over* its loss of love and displeasure to Christ (2 Cor. 7:8-10),
- that it is *turning away* from sin and *returning to* its past life of love,
- that it will, by God's grace, *take appropriate action* (2 Cor. 7:8-12).

The Ephesians could not restore their first love without repenting—the Lord would not allow it. The lesson here is

> **Repentance is at the heart of what the Ephesian believers must do to restore their first love.**

that sin must always be dealt with; it cannot be ignored. Repentance is at the heart of what the Ephesian believers must do to restore their first love. If they neglected Christ's call to repent, they would face divine judgment: "If not, I will come to you and remove your lampstand from its place, unless you repent" (Rev. 2:5).

Do the Works You Did at First

After "remember" and "repent," the third imperative command is "do the works you did at first." Literally the text reads, "And do the first works." The word *first* reminds us of its earlier appearance in Revelation 2:4, "you have abandoned the love you had at first." Genuine repentance produces "fruit in keeping with repentance" (Matt. 3:8; also 2 Cor. 7:10-11). Thus, Jesus points them back to their first works, which sprang from their first love.

In the case of the Ephesians, returning to their first works means returning to their former state and eagerly seeking to reengage in the deeds of love they once had done but had abandoned. Jesus is not simply telling them to do more works—they have works (Rev. 2:2)—but to do the works they did at first. It may be that their present "toil" and "patient endurance" were largely confined to stopping false teachers, preserving sound doctrine from attack, and facing opposition from a hostile society.

As the Ephesian believers gradually abandoned their first love, they also abandoned, or greatly minimized, certain acts of love, kindness, compassion, care, hospitality, and prayer.[15] Loss of love always has adverse consequences on a church's works, conduct, attitudes, and activities. The Ephesians worked

---

15 Rom. 12:9-21; 1 Tim. 5:10; 1 John 3:11-18.

hard and endured, but there were missing elements of their work that needed to be restored.

To the church at Ephesus, it is good news that repentance secures the Lord's forgiveness and help. Christ will "supply them with the oil of fresh love"[16] for their lamp to shine bright again. He wants nothing more than their love to be revived and to grow stronger. He wants them to love like they first loved.

For us, as for the Ephesians, the fire of love can be rekindled. Lives can be rededicated to Christ. The Holy Spirit can breathe new life into prayer, Bible study, evangelism, worship, and fellowship with one another. We can more fully know and abide in the love that God has for us (1 John 4:16). We can more consistently walk in love as Christ loved us and gave Himself up for us (Eph. 5:2). Practical ways of doing that are provided in the next part of this book.

---

[16] Robert Tuck, *A Homiletic Commentary* (New York: Funk & Wagnalls, n.d.), 9: 451.

Part Two

How To Cultivate Love

Let us consider how to stir up one another to love and good works.
Heb. 10:24

The Lord's rebuke to the church in Ephesus is a strong warning that a church can work hard, fight heresy, persevere, teach sound doctrine, and yet, because of a lack of love, be in danger of divine discipline. No matter how impressive a church may appear to be on the outside—a magnificent building, huge congregation, large staff, big budget, dynamic teaching, outstanding missions program, and awesome music—it may still be dying within from a lack of love (1 Cor. 13:1-3).

Love is vital to the spiritual health of the individual believer and to the local church, so cultivating love within the church body is a subject dear to my heart. I grieve over churches that have lost touch with the New Testament spirit and practices of love. I mourn for churches that are arrogant because of their sound doctrine but are soundly asleep in regard to their love (1 Cor. 13:4). I also mourn for churches that are proud of their love but are doctrinally asleep. It is disillusioning to see churches that, because of distorted views of love, refuse to discipline unrepentant sinning members. It is distressing to see self-satisfied Christians who refuse to grow in love. I can hardly believe it when I see believers fight with one another like dirty street fighters (suing, slandering, and hating one another) and show little regard for the behaviors of love described in the Bible (1 Cor. 13:4-7).

Every believer should be concerned about the loss of love in the family of God. Although God ultimately is the one who keeps us in his love and motivates us to love,[1] there is also a human side of the equation. Scripture directs

---

[1] John 15:9; Rom. 5:5; 8:35-39; Gal. 5:22; Jude 1.

all believers to pursue love, keep ourselves in the love of God, abide in Christ's love, walk in love as Christ loved, and consider how to stir up one another to love and good deeds.[2] Thus it is vital to our church communities and to the spiritual health of individual believers that we know how to cultivate and protect love.

The nurture and practice of love is a life and death issue to the local church. We do not want the Lord to say of us, "I have this against you." It is our responsibility, then, both individually and corporately to cultivate and guard love. We must learn how to grow in love as individuals and as a church family. We must motivate ourselves and others to love "in deed and in truth" (1 John 3:18). And when love is dying, we must revive and restore the pursuit of love.

---

[2] 1 Cor. 14:1; Jude 21; John 15:9; Eph. 5:2; Heb. 10:24.

Chapter One

Study Love

Since the love we seek to imitate is Christ's love, there can be no better starting point than to study what God says about love in his Word, the Bible. It is the standard for defining divine love and for correcting our false notions about love, yet few believers realize all that the Bible teaches about love.

In the *English Standard Version* of the Bible, the different forms of the word *love* appear almost a thousand times.[3] In addition, the concept of love occurs in the Bible many times when the actual word itself is not used. The topic of love is so vast because God is love—the author, definer, and rewarder of love. So it is only natural that love permeates his Word.

If you want to pursue love, you must read and study what God says about love in his written Word. You will then grow in the knowledge of love and in the knowledge of God and Christ whom we are to love above all others. Nothing but God's Word and Spirit can awaken our desire to love and transform our sinfully selfish hearts to love as Christ loves. If the Scriptures don't convince us of the importance of love and God's requirements to love, then nothing will.

> **If you want to pursue love, you must read and study what God says about love in his written Word.**

Henry Moorhouse and the Study of Love

The story of Henry Moorhouse's influence on the great 19th century evangelist, Dwight L. Moody, is a wonderful illustration of the importance of

---

[3] I have included in this general number the word "steadfast love" (Hebrew, *hesed*), when translated as *steadfast love* or *love*.

studying biblical love.[4] Henry Moorhouse was a young, itinerate, British evangelist. His method for preaching the gospel was to take a subject and study it from Genesis to Revelation. He then was able to preach his subject from the whole of Scripture. His messages were a rich banquet of scriptural content skillfully complemented by fitting illustrations that clarified the meaning of the Scriptures for his unbelieving listeners.

Of all the subjects Moorhouse enjoyed studying and preaching, his favorite was the love of God as proclaimed in John 3:16: "For God so loved the world, that he gave his only Son, that whoever believes in him should not perish but have eternal life." So when Henry Moorhouse first visited America and preached at Moody's church in Chicago, he preached seven straight messages on John 3:16 in one week! Using the entire Bible, Moorhouse took his audience on a thrilling exploration of God's amazing love.

Everything Moorhouse said that week was backed by Scripture. As a result of his extensive use of the Bible in his preaching, people started to carry their Bibles to church for the first time. His preaching proved to be so Spirit-empowered that the crowds grew larger each day. His preaching initiated a spiritual awakening of love in the church. Even Moody confessed that he couldn't hold back the tears as he listened to Moorhouse hammer away at verse after verse from Scripture on God's love for lost sinners displayed in Christ's death.

Until this time, Moody had preached only on divine judgment for sinners, not on God's love for sinners. But as a result of Moorhouse's seven sermons on John 3:16, Moody "was never the same man."[5] Although Moody at first had disliked Moorhouse, they soon became close, life-long friends. Henry Moorhouse, who looked like a seventeen-year-old, beardless teenager and stood no taller than Moody's shoulders, was not afraid to urge the imposing Moody to study his Bible more and preach more scripturally focused messages. Moody responded to this urging positively and Henry became Moody's teacher.

---

[4] It is estimated that Moody preached the gospel to more than a 100 million people, traveled more than a million miles, and lead hundreds of thousands of people to the knowledge of Christ, all of this before the days of planes, cars, radio, and TV (Lyle W. Dorsett, *A Passion for Souls: The Life of D. L. Moody* [Chicago: Moody, 1997], 139).

[5] Dorsett, *A Passion for Souls*, 139.

Moorhouse's example of personal study and powerful preaching on the love of God in Christ motivated Moody to study what the Bible said about love. Moody was amazed by his experience with the study of biblical love:

> I took up that word "Love," and I do not know how many weeks I spent in studying the passages in which it occurs, *till at last I could not help loving people!* (Italics mine.) I had been feeding on Love so long that I was anxious to do everybody good I came in contact with.
>
> I got full of it. It ran out my fingers. You take up the subject of love in the *Bible!* You will get so full of it that all you have got to do is to open your lips, and a flood of the Love of God flows out upon the meeting. There is no use trying to do church work without love. A doctor, a lawyer, may do good work without love, but God's work cannot be done without love.[6]

The Bible is unparalleled in its claims and demands of love. All that it says about love will amaze you. If you accept Moody's challenge to "take up the subject of love in the Bible," you, too, will find that you want to do good to everyone. Love will flow out of your mouth and your fingers. You will want to be a better example of Christlike love.

And, like Moorhouse, your passion for understanding and growing in God's love will become insatiable. In fact, John 3:16 became Moorhouse's signature message. Even on his deathbed, Moorhouse said to a friend, "If it were the Lord's will to raise me up again, I should like to preach more the text, 'God so loved the world.' "[7] Days later he died at the young age of forty. Engraved on his memorial is John 3:16.

Getting Started in the Study of Love

A quick, simple way to begin to explore what the Bible says about love is to read the biblical texts on love in the appendix of this book (Appendix B: Fifty

---

[6] Richard Ellsworth Day, Bush Aglow: *The Life Story of Dwight Lyman Moody, Commoner of Northfield* (Philadelphia, PA: The Judson Press, 1936), 146.

[7] John Macpherson, *Henry Moorhouse: The English Evangelist* (London: Morgan and Scott, n.d.), 130.

Key Texts on Love). These passages will give you a broad overview of the biblical landscape of love. But don't just read through them quickly; take the time to think and meditate on biblical, Christlike love.[8]

Another way to study love is to look up verses that include the word love in a Bible concordance or software program. Read the verses in context, then categorize each one according to specific topics that will help you remember the Bible's teaching on love. For example, John 17:24 provides invaluable insight into the Father's love for the Son. Additional examples of categories may include:

God is Love
The Father's Love for the Son
The Son's Love for the Father
The Holy Spirit and Love
God's Love for Israel
God's Unfailing Love
Jesus Christ's Love for His People
The Believer's Love for God
The Believer's Love for Christ
The Believer's Love for Other Believers
The Believer's Love for the Lost
Love Relationships Among People (husband-wife, parent-child,
   friends, leader-followers, etc.)
Growth in Love
The Commands of Love
The Nature of Love
The Importance of Love
Love and Prayer
Love and Obedience

As you read about love, keep in mind that our Lord teaches that the first and

---

8 Martyn Lloyd-Jones adds, "Love is something which can be contemplated.... If love does not make you think, it is not love; it is a purely physical instinct. Love enjoys ruminating, dwelling upon, looking at, dissecting, analyzing and considering.... Love is to be studied, and the more you study it the more you enjoy it" (*The Unsearchable Riches of Christ: An Exposition of Ephesians 3:1 to 21* [Grand Rapids: Baker, 1979], 232-233).

greatest commandment, and the chief duty of life, is to love God supremely above self, others, or all material things.[9] All human love finds its proper place and order in life only when love for the eternal Creator-God is first and foremost. To love any created being or material object above the Creator is idolatry and a perversion of love.

> *"There is no use trying to do church work without love. A doctor, a lawyer, may do good work without love, but God's work cannot be done without love."*
> —D. L. MOODY

The second commandment to love is inseparable from the first: "You shall love your neighbor as yourself." Love for God and neighbor are the sum of all God's commandments, all ethical behavior, all religious service, and all true inner spirituality. The paramount importance of these two love commandments is emphatically stressed by Christ himself when he says:

On these two commandments depend all the Law and the Prophets. (Matt. 22:40)

There is no other commandment greater than these. (Mark 12:31)

Of course, the study of what the Bible says about love is not a one-time study, but a life-long learning process. Learning of God's love in Christ and God's love for us is a never-ending pursuit. It is one of the most interesting and thrilling subjects in all of Scripture. By saturating your mind with biblical love, you will know what God requires of you and you will grow in love. You will also be able to guard yourself from the loss of love and be better equipped to urge others to love.

After you have studied biblical love, encourage others to do the same. Start a small group study on love and use the study guide provided in this book or the study guide to my book, *A Christian Leader's Guide to Leading with Love*.[10] (Although that book is written primarily to leaders, anyone can use it and profit from its expositions of Scripture.) Getting people in your church to gather together to study biblical love will greatly encourage a spirit of love in your church. The study of biblical love is an important way to "pursue love" (1 Cor. 14:1) and "stir up one another to love and good works" (Heb. 10:24).

---

[9] Deut. 6:4-5; Matt. 22:34-40; Mark 12:28-34; Luke 10:25-42.

[10] Alexander Strauch, *A Christian Leader's Guide to Leading with Love* (Littleton, CO Lewis and Roth, 2006).

Chapter Two

Pray for Love

It is one thing to study love, but quite another to put into practice what we learn. We can, however, learn a great deal about living in love from the way in which the apostles encouraged the outpouring of Christ's love that was evident in the first churches. The apostles were far more concerned about love than we tend to be. The New Testament shows us that they *taught* the believers what Christ taught on love; *exhorted* their readers to practice Christ's love; *modeled* Christ's love for their converts to follow; *warned* about loving this present world more than Christ; and *prayed* for their converts to grow in Christlike love. We will explore each of these points, starting with prayer.

One reason we see little growth in love in our churches is because we exert little effort in praying for it. We are naturally selfish people who simply cannot, at least in our own strength, walk in love as Christ did. If ever

> **There can be no revival of love without persevering prayer.**

we are to love as Christ loved, we must pray for the Holy Spirit's enablement. There can be no revival of love without persevering prayer. George Müller, a remarkable man of prayer, understood the necessity of ongoing prayer:

> The great fault of the children of God is, *they do not continue in prayer; they do not go on praying; they do not persevere.* If they desire anything for God's glory, they should pray until they get it.[11]

The New Testament provides examples of prayers for growth in love. Paul, for instance, prayed that his converts would grow in their knowledge of God's

---

[11]   Roger Steer, *George Müller: Delighted in God* (1975; reprint ed., Fern, Scotland: Christian Focus, 1997), 222.

love for them, in their knowledge of Christ's sacrificial love on the cross, and in their love for one another and for all people. Our examination of these prayers will be both instructive and challenging to our prayer life.

Pray to Know Christ's Love

In one of the greatest prayers recorded in the New Testament, Paul prays that God would enable believers, by the Holy Spirit's power, to grasp the vast, incomprehensible nature of Christ's love:

> I bow my knees before the Father...that...he may grant you to be strengthened with power through his Spirit in your inner being,... that you...may have strength to comprehend with all the saints what is the breadth and length and height and depth [of Christ's love], and to know the love of Christ that surpasses knowledge. (Eph. 3:14-19)

Although Christ's love "surpasses knowledge," it is still something we are to continually seek to understand.[12] The great truth we must come back to again and again throughout life is this: *Not that we loved Christ, but that he first loved us and gave up his life on the cross for our sins.* It is a worthwhile task then, to pray diligently to know the love of Christ our Savior.[13]

To know Christ's love—not only intellectually, but also experientially and intimately—is life-changing. C.T. Studd, pioneer missionary to China, India, and Africa, understood the truth of Christ's sacrificial love and responded by declaring, "If Jesus Christ be God and died for me, then no sacrifice can be too great for me to make for Him."[14] The truth of Christ's love inspired John

---

12 Commenting on our passage, Martyn Lloyd-Jones writes, "We must never fall into the error of imagining that because we are Christians we therefore know all about the love of God. Most of us are but as children paddling at the edge of an ocean; there are abysmal depths in this love of God of which we know nothing. The Apostle is praying that these Ephesians, and we with them, may go out into the depths and the deeps, and discover things which we have never even imagined" (*The Unsearchable Riches of Christ*, 207).

13 Ceslaus Spicq comments, "The whole Christian life consists in clinging to his love and living in it" (*Agape in the New Testament* [London: Herder, 1965], 2: 373).

14 Norman Grubb, *C.T. Studd: Cricketer and Pioneer* (Fort Washington, PA: Christian Literature Crusade, 1933), 132. C. T. Studd's father was converted under the preaching of D. L. Moody.

The secret of the early Christians,
the early Protestants, Puritans and Methodists
was that they were taught about
the love of Christ,
and they became filled with a knowledge of it.
Once a man has the love of Christ in his heart
you need not train him to witness;
he will do it.
He will know the power, the constraint, the motive;
everything is already there.
It is a plain lie to suggest that people
who regard this knowledge
of the love of Christ as the supreme thing
are useless, unhealthy mystics.
The servants of God who have most adorned
the life and the history of the Christian Church
have always been men who have realized
that this is the most important thing of all,
and they have spent hours in prayer
seeking His face and enjoying His love.
The man who knows the love of Christ in his heart
can do more in one hour
than the busy type of man can do in a century.
God forbid that we should ever
make of activity an end in itself.
Let us realize that the motive must come first,
and that the motive must ever be
the love of Christ.

(D. Martyn Lloyd-Jones, *The Unsearchable Riches of Christ*, 253)

Stott to paint this thought-provoking word picture: "The cross is the blazing fire at which the flame of our love is kindled."[15]

The more we understand and appreciate Christ's sacrificial love at Calvary, the greater will be our love for God and our neighbor. Indeed, the logic of Scripture is this: "If God so loved us, we also ought to love one another . . . We love because he first loved us" (1 John 4:11, 19). Let us, then, never cease to pray for a deeper understanding and appreciation of Christ's sacrificial love that will help us love him more.

One practical way to invigorate your prayers for greater appreciation of Christ's love or more love for Christ is by singing your prayers. You can sing as prayers many hymns and contemporary praise choruses about Christ's love, love for Christ, and love for one another. For example, you can sing the following hymn as a prayer for more love for Christ:

> More love to Thee, O Christ, more love to Thee!
> Hear Thou the prayer I make
> On bended knee;
> This is my earnest plea:
> More love, O Christ, to Thee!
> More love to Thee,
> More love to Thee!
>
> Once earthly joy I craved,
> Sought peace and rest;
> Now Thee alone I seek—
> Give what is best;
> This all my prayer shall be:
> More love, O Christ, to Thee!
> More love to Thee,
> More love to Thee!

(*More Love to Thee*, by Elizabeth Prentiss)

It is spiritually energizing to sing of Christ's love or to ask in song for more love. Why not choose several of your favorite songs of love for Christ and

---

15 John R. W. Stott, *What Christ Thinks of the Church: An Exposition of Revelation 1-3* (Grand Rapids: Baker, 2003), 33.

Christ's love for us and use them as prayers and aids to your prayers? If you heed the advice of the Psalmist, "Come into his presence with singing" (Ps. 100:2), you will discover singing to be an enormous aid to invigorating your prayer life. You will soon be rejoicing with the Psalmist, "I will sing aloud of your steadfast love in the morning" (Ps. 59:16); "I will sing of the steadfast love of the Lord, forever" (Ps. 89:1).

Pray to Love Others More

Love is not static but dynamic. Love is to be increasing, not diminishing. So Paul specifically prayed that his converts would not only grow in love but would overflow in love for one another and for all people:

> May the Lord make you increase and abound in love for one anoth-er and for all [people], as we do for you. (1 Thess. 3:12)

> And it is my prayer [to God] that your love may abound more and more. (Phil. 1:9)

In a similar vein, Jude also prayed for his readers,

> May…love be multiplied to you. (Jude 2)

These Spirit-inspired prayers are wonderful models to pray for ourselves and for others.

To see continual growth in love among believers delighted Paul's heart. The newly planted church in Thessalonica was a bright beacon of Christian love. In fact, we see in this new church an example of *first love* on display. Yet Paul exhorts these loving believers to excel even more in their love: "But we urge you, brothers, to do this more and more" (1 Thess. 4:10). In his second letter to the Thessalonians, Paul gladly acknowledges that "the love of every one of you for one another is increasing" (2 Thess. 1:3).

In their commentary on 1 & 2 Thessalonians, W. E. Vine and C. F. Hogg remind us that,

> The Christian may not rest in any measure of attainment, howev-er great, but must always be stretching out after a closer approxi-mation to the standard, which is Christ.[16]

---

16 C. F. Hogg and W. E. Vine, *The Epistles to the Thessalonians* (Fincastle, VA: Bible Study Classics, n.d.), 123-124.

The reason believers are never to stop growing in our capacity to love others is because love is a fruit of the Holy Spirit, and the Holy Spirit wants to produce abundant fruit in us (Gal. 5:22). He wants us to love as Christ loved. In the church at Ephesus, however, the fruit of love was shriveling and dying out. The believers were self-satisfied and complacent about loving others. Whenever Christians stop abounding in the fruit of love or think they love enough, they are on the road to becoming like the church in Ephesus. They are no longer growing in love or producing the fruit of Christian love.[17]

Growth in love does not happen overnight. I once heard a country preacher tell how he discovered the limitless capacity of love. When he was in his early twenties and still quite immature, he and his wife had their first child. He loved his newborn baby girl so much that he couldn't imagine having a second child. He was a completely devoted father. He carried her picture with him and showed it to everyone. He couldn't wait to get home from work to see and hold his baby girl. He didn't think he ever could love anyone else as much as he loved her. He thought he had no more love to give.

After a period of time, his wife suggested that they have another child. He protested, "But dear, I don't have any more love to give. I've poured out all my love on our little girl. It's not possible to love any more!"

> It "is of the very essence of love ... to overflow."
> —WILLIAM HENDRIKSEN

Well, his wife prevailed and a year later they had a beautiful baby boy. Quickly the father discovered he loved his new baby boy as much as his little girl. Now he loved two children equally.

After a year or so, his wife said, "We should have another child."

Again he protested, "Sweetheart, I don't have any more love in me. I love these two children with all the love I have. I'm loved out."

His wife prevailed and they had a third child, another boy. When the third child arrived, the father found that he had plenty of love. He loved the third child as much as the other two. Finally he understood that he wasn't going to run out of love.

The same is true of us. As believers, indwelt by the Holy Spirit, we have an immense capacity to love all people—even our enemies and those who are

---

17 Donald S. Whitney is right when he says, "If you are growing in your love for others—especially in your love for Christians—then you are growing as a Christian" (*Ten Questions to Diagnose Your Spiritual Health* [Colorado Springs: NavPress, 2001], 41).

unlovely or disagreeable. We have the power to love as Jesus loved and to continue to abound in love throughout life. Commentator William Hendriksen states the principle well: it "is of the very essence of love ... to overflow."[18]

We all have to admit, however, that growth in love is a struggle. "The best believers," writes Maurice Roberts, "find their progress slow and their attainments meager."[19] This is why we need to pray continually for God's help. Paul says that the Thessalonian believers were "taught by God to love one another" (1 Thess. 4:9). He who is the source of love is also the best teacher of love, and he has given to his Spirit the unique work of inspiring and prompting love within us.[20]

So, is your love growing and overflowing? Or is your love shrinking and dying? The more we see how inherently and perversely selfish we are, the more we recognize our need to ask God to help us to love. The more we understand God's demands of love, the more we realize our need to pray for a heart of joyful obedience. The more we see how little love we truly have for Christ and others, the more we recognize our need to pray for more love. Ask God to be your teacher. Ask him to teach you how to grow and abound in love. Ask and keep asking!

Our battle with self-centered living demands constant confession and prayer. Prayer is one of the key means by which God works in us and accomplishes his purposes in our lives. Only by prayer and the Lord's grace can we grow and overflow with love and have victory over self-centered living. Let these solemn words of Maurice Roberts ring in our ears and move us to pray:

> Then let every Christian take up the duty of Christian love with tenfold seriousness. Our life's work must be to call down heaven's help upon ourselves that we may bend towards the great command to love one another.[21]

---

18 William Hendriksen, *Colossians and Philemon*, NTC (Grand Rapids: Baker, 1964), 158.

19 Maurice Roberts, "The Supreme Grace of Christian Love," *The Banner of Truth* (February, 1989): 3.

20 Rom 5:5; 15:30; Gal. 5:22.

21 Roberts, "The Supreme Grace of Christian Love," 4.

Praying Strengthens Love Relationships

Communication is essential in every good relationship. Those we love, we seek to be near and speak with regularly. In contrast, distance and infrequent communication hurt relationships. This is true not only in our human relationships, but in our love relationship with God.

> **I cannot encourage you enough to make praying for love a regular part of your prayer life.**

No one has ever enjoyed such an intimate relationship with God as did Jesus Christ, and he was preeminently a man of prayer. Likewise, the time we spend in prayer strengthens our love relationship with our Father in heaven. Through prayer, we draw close to God and enter into his very presence—the thing he desires most (Heb. 4:16; 10:19). So if you want your love relationship with God to grow, you must seek his presence, sing his praises, read his word, and respond to him in prayer.

Love for God naturally overflows in love for others. One way we express our love for others is through intercessory prayer. Paul loved his converts and prayed for them night and day. Jesus loved his disciples and prayed for them (John 17). Even now, he continues to pray for his people.[22] The Bible tells us that we are to express love for our enemies by praying for them (Matt. 5:44). So prayer is an act of "genuine love" (Rom. 12:9, 12). A person who is growing in love is a person who is praying to God for the needs of others, and a person who intercedes is a person who is growing in love.

I cannot encourage you enough to make praying for love a regular part of your prayer life. Pray for increasing knowledge of God's love in Christ. Pray to excel more in love for others. Pray with others for growth in love. In your church prayer meeting or in your small group study, pray for more love for Christ and for a lost, suffering world. As you pray, "May the Lord make you increase and abound in love for one another and for all" (1 Thess. 3:12).

---

[22] Rom. 8:34; Heb. 7:25; 1 John 2:1.

Chapter Three

Teach Love

During Christ's public teaching ministry on earth, he taught his followers stirring new truths about love.[23] And during the final hours before his death, at the last Passover meal, Jesus revealed some of his most profound teaching on love.[24] He knew that if the disciples were to survive without him and represent him properly to the world, they must learn how to love one another as he had loved them.

Following their Lord's example, the apostles deemed it necessary to teach and exhort the first churches about love. They prayed earnestly for their converts to grow in love and diligently taught them to live a life of love that was patterned after Christ's love (Eph. 5:2). Thus the New Testament letters are full of inspiring instructions on love and challenging exhortations to love.

Believers today still need to be taught how to love. Just as was true in New Testament times, we need regular teaching on the biblical principles of love. We need a passion for teaching and obeying the whole counsel of God on love. We need to be exhorted to practice love, not just talk about it. We need to hear teaching on the major New Testament passages on love.[25] Such biblical instruction on love would significantly improve the love expressed in our local churches. Toward that end, I urge you to consider the following topics on love that must be taught in order to nurture the growth of love in our churches.

---

[23] Matt. 5:43-48; 6:24; 10:37-38; 22:34-40; Mark 12:28-34; Luke 6:27-36; 10:25-42; John 13-17.

[24] Love (both the noun *apagē* and verb *agapaō*) appears thirty-three times in Christ's farewell discourse (John 13-17). In contrast, the words occur twelve times in John 1-12.

[25] Matt. 5:43-48; 22:34-40; John 13:34-35; 1 Cor. 12:31-13:13; Rom. 8:35-39; 12:9-21; 13:8-10; 14:15; Eph. 3:18-19; 5:1-2, 25; 1 John 3:16-18; 4:7-5:3; Rev. 2:4.

Fifteen Descriptions of Love

People frequently sing and speak about love without ever describing what they mean by love. One of the most popular songs of the 1960s was the Beatles' *All You Need Is Love.* The word *love* is repeated thirty-nine times throughout the song and the phrase "all you need is love" twelve times. The song is catchy, and it does make a point: we all need love. The problem, however, is that it doesn't tell us what love is or why we need it. But in the Bible, God does tell us the truth about love, and that is what people need to be taught.

In an age of biblical illiteracy, believers need to know the truth about love. Believers need to be taught the fifteen descriptions of love in 1 Corinthians 13, the great love chapter of the New Testament. When I was preaching in another country recently, I gave several messages on 1 Corinthians 13:4-7. When I finished speaking, an older man who had been a leading preacher in that country for many years came up to me and said he had never heard a series of sermons on the fifteen descriptions of love. Given the vital importance of love and the need to know what love is, he thought the lack of teaching on the subject was a terrible oversight on the part of preachers such as himself.

God, however, has not overlooked the importance of teaching on love. Although the Bible doesn't give a formal dictionary definition of love, it describes in detail what love does and doesn't do (1 Corinthians 13:4-7). It also gives us the example of Christ's total, self-sacrificing love for others and his loving obedience to the Father as a description of love.

The love descriptions of 1 Corinthians 13 set before us an objective standard of love. The scriptural standard of love is a test of our notions of love and instructs us in how to conduct ourselves in a loving manner in marriage, church, and society. The fifteen principles of love can be summarized as follows:

Love is
1. Patient
2. Kind

Love is not

	The Positive Counterpart
3. Envious	Rejoices in the blessings of others
4. Boastful	Promotes and praises others
5. Arrogant	Is humble and modest
6. Rude	Promotes proper decorum
7. Selfish	Is occupied with the good of others
8. Easily Angered	Is calm and slow to anger
9. Resentful	Forgives

10. Does not rejoice at wrongdoing, but   11. Rejoices with the truth

Love
12. Bears all things
13. Believes all things
14. Hopes all things
15. Endures all things

Understanding and putting into practice the principles of love is so important that whenever I perform a marriage I give the new couple an assignment on their wedding day! I ask them to take the first fifteen weeks of their marriage to study the fifteen descriptions of love. I ask them to dedicate one week to each description. Throughout that week, they are to study, memorize, meditate on, and discuss ways to practically implement each positive virtue of love and avoid the negative qualities (the vices of selfishness). This assignment, which expands their understanding of true biblical love, could benefit anyone—married or single.

Love in the Christian Life
Since we live in a society that worships at the altars of personal self-fulfillment, radical individualism, personal rights and freedom, and privacy, it is crucial to teach that the supreme duty of the believer is to love God first and foremost. Believers need practical, biblical guidance on what love for God looks like and how we are to love. We need to know the inseparable connection between loving God and obeying God as a response of love.[26]

Believers need to be taught that the Christian life is to be characterized by Christ's total, self-giving love: "Walk in love, as Christ loved us and gave himself up for us (Eph. 5:2)." Our daily walk in love is to be patterned after Christ's costly, sacrificial love for others: "By this we know love, that he laid down his life for us, and we ought to lay down our lives for the brothers" (1 John 3:16).

John Eadie's understanding of what it means to walk in love bears repeating:

> "Walk in love." Every step is to be one of love. The whole tenor and course of life are to be characterized by love—not only on the

---

[26] Ex. 20:6; Deut. 10:12-13; 11:1, 13, 22; 19:9; 30:16, 19-20; John 14:15, 21, 31; 15:10; 1 John 2:5; 5:3; 2 John 6.

Sabbath, but on every day; not only in the sanctuary, but in the house, the workshop.... [27]

And Benjamin B. Warfield captures succinctly the profound truth of the Christian life of love when he writes, "Self-sacrificing love is thus made the essence of the Christian life."[28]

The Christian life, then, should be characterized by obedience to God's Word and costly, sacrificial service for the welfare of others. J. I. Packer provides a marvelous summation of love and the Christian life:

> The measure and test of love to God is wholehearted and unqualified obedience.... the measure and test of love to our neighbors is laying down our lives for them.... This sacrificial love involves giving, spending, and impoverishing ourselves up to the limit for their well-being.[29]

This is the kind of Christian life God intends us to live. It is imitating our heavenly Father and thus imitating his Son's love:

> Therefore be imitators of God, as beloved children. And walk in love, as Christ loved us and gave himself up for us, as a fragrant offering and sacrifice to God." (Eph. 5:1-2)

Love in the Christian Home

With Christian families divorcing and breaking apart in record numbers, we need to teach the centrality of costly, sacrificial love in Christian marriage and the home. The Scripture directs husbands to love their "wives, as Christ loved the church and gave himself up for her" (Eph. 5:25; Col. 3:19) and instructs older women to "train the young women to love their husbands and children" (Titus 2:4). We must clearly teach that the standard of love God sets for

---

[27] John Eadie, *Divine Love: A Series of Doctrinal, Practical and Experimental Discourses* (1856; Birmingham, AL: Solid Ground Christian Books, 2005), 273.

[28] Benjamin Breckenridge Warfield, "The Emotional Life of Our Lord," in *The Person and Work of Christ* (Philadelphia: Presbyterian and Reformed, 1950), 64.

[29] J. I. Packer, *Concise Theology* (Wheaton: Tyndale, 1993), 181-182.

Christian husbands is nothing less than Christ's total, self-giving love. *Thus the Christian home should be characterized by Christ's unselfish, giving love—a love that is initiated by the husband.*

Two missionaries traveled to a church on an isolated Pacific island to teach and encourage the believers. When the missionaries arrived, the local church elders requested that the missionaries teach on women's submission and proper clothing. Knowing the people well, the missionaries said instead, "We are going to teach the men how to love their wives as Christ sacrificially loved the Church and gave himself up for her."

Although the elders initially didn't see the need for such teaching, they trusted the missionaries' judgment and soon understood the wisdom in first teaching the men how to love their wives as Christ sacrificially loved the Church and gave himself up for her. Male selfishness (whether expressed by domination or passivity in the marriage) is often the chief problem in marriages. So in God's plan, when Christ's self-giving, self-sacrificing love is evident in the husband's relationship with his wife, it sets in order the entire atmosphere of the Christian home.

> "The measure and test of love to God is wholehearted and unqualified obedience.... the measure and test of love to our neighbors is laying down our lives for them...."
> —J. I. PACKER

Marriage provides opportunities for daily practice in the cultivation of Christlike love (Eph. 5:25-33). It exposes our deplorable self-centeredness and desperate need for growth in Christlike love. The home is the best testing ground for the kind of love described in 1 Corinthians 13:4-7. It is a tragic situation when some believers show abundant love to people at church or in the neighborhood, but fail to express the same love to their spouse or children. This should not be. Love begins at home. Therefore, I encourage you to do what some husbands and wives have done (and done successfully, I might add): pray specifically for more Christlike love for your spouse and children.

Love in the Local Church Family

The local church is a divinely created family in which we learn to love as Christ loved. The local church is to be a close-knit family of brothers and sisters who are totally committed to displaying God's love by loving and caring for one another. The standard of love set for the local church is best explained by

John: "By this we know love, that he laid down his life for us, and we ought to lay down our lives for the brothers" (1 John 3:16).

Believers cannot encourage one another to love if they don't meet together regularly as a church family. This is why the writer of Hebrews exhorts his readers to think creatively of ways to "stir up one another to love,"[30] and warns them about neglecting "to meet together, as is the habit of some" (Heb. 10:25). Our growth in love is not just an individual exercise. Love requires both a subject and an object, thus love is a corporate learning experience. We grow in love by engagement with other people, not in isolation from them.

Christians cannot develop love by sitting at home alone on the couch watching TV preachers or by attending a weekly, one-hour church service. It is only through participation in "the household of God," the local church (1 Tim. 3:15), with all of its weaknesses and faults, that love is taught, modeled, learned, tested, practiced, and matured. By dealing with difficult people, facing painful conflicts, forgiving hurts and injustices, reconciling estranged relationships, and helping needy members, our love is tested and matures.

> **The local church truly is "a spiritual workshop for the development of agape love."**
> —PAUL E. BILLHEIMER

One simply cannot grow in love without the stresses and strains of life together in the household of God, the local church. The local church truly is "a spiritual workshop for the development of *agape* love" and "one of the very best laboratories in which individual believers may discover their real spiritual emptiness and begin to grow in *agape* love."[31] If you are not a participating member of a local church, then you are not in God's school of love.

Love and the Local Church Body

Believers also need to be taught that responsibility for the church's growth in love (or its loss of love) is not just the responsibility of the church leaders; it is the responsibility of every member of the church family. When the writer

---

[30] Commenting on Hebrew 10:24, Donald Guthrie writes, "It seems to suggest that loving one another will not just happen. It needs to be worked at, even provoked, in the same way as good works" (*The Letter to the Hebrews,* TNTC [Grand Rapids: Eerdmans, 1983], 215).

[31] Paul E. Billheimer, *Love Covers* (Fort Washington, PA: Christian Literature Crusade, 1981), 34.

of Hebrews says, "consider how to stir up one another to love and good works" (Heb. 10:24), he addresses the whole believing community. In fact, all the biblical commands to love one another are directed to the entire congregation, not just a few key leaders. From the perspective of the New Testament writers, every member of the believing community is responsible for encouraging, praying for, exhorting, serving, admonishing, teaching, building up, caring for, and loving one another.[32] Indeed, Scripture teaches us that all believers are priests, saints, and servants of God.

To make this daunting task possible, God has given each individual believer a spiritual gift to use in building up the body of Christ.[33] Each member is divinely empowered by Christ to serve the body of Christ, and each has a part to play in the life of the church body. The church grows properly only as each member actively contributes his or her part to the growth of the body. Thus the whole believing community participates in the process of building up the church.

> *"My business is to love others, not to seek that others love me."*
> —ROBERT CLEAVER CHAPMAN

However, as the Scripture makes abundantly clear, all gifts and services in the body must be exercised "in love" in order for the church to grow in a healthy manner (Eph. 4:16).[34] Love is thus an indispensable element to every believer's gift, work, and relationship in the body of Christ. So don't wait around for people to love you; start loving and serving others. I urge you to follow the example of Robert Cleaver Chapman who said, "My business is to love others, not to seek that others love me."[35] Put into practice the principle of love that says, "whatever you wish that oth-

---

[32] 1 Cor. 12:25; Rom. 15:14; Gal. 5:13; Col. 3:16; 1 Thess. 4:18; 5:11; Heb. 3:13; 10:24-25; James 5:16; 1 Peter 4:10; 1 John 4:7.

[33] Rom. 12:6-8; 1 Cor. 12:1-31; 14:1-40; Eph. 4:7-16; 1 Peter 4:10-11.

[34] Commenting on Ephesians 4:16, Peter T. O'Brien says, "Clearly the whole body is involved in this process of building [the church], not simply those who are leaders or who have special ministries…. The 'spiritually gifted community is not only distinguished by its full possession of gifts through which divine energy flows, but it is also marked by its divine nature'. Love thus becomes the criterion for an assessment of the church's true growth. Even the fullest demonstration of gifts has no spiritual value if love is lacking (cf. 1 Cor. 13)" (*The Letter to the Ephesians,* PNTC [Grand Rapids: Eerdmans, 1999], 316).

[35] Robert L. Peterson and Alexander Strauch, *Agape Leadership: Lessons in Spiritual Leadership from the Life of R.C. Chapman* (Littleton, CO: Lewis and Roth, 1991), 21.

ers would do to you, do also to them" (Matt. 7:12). Don't neglect your responsibility to love and stir up others to love.

Love for All People

Many Christians mistakenly consider themselves to be loving people simply because they love their Christian friends and relatives. They love those who agree with them and remain in their circle of fellowship, but if someone disagrees with them or leaves their church, they stop loving and start attacking. Jonathan Edwards describes such Christians in this way:

> They are full of dear affections to some, and full of bitterness toward others. They are knit to their own party, them that approve of them, love them and admire them; but are fierce against those that oppose and dislike them.[36]

This kind of love is not Christian love. Jesus taught that loving those who love us is nothing out of the ordinary. It is natural to love those who are friendly and agreeable with us, but Jesus says,

> If you love those who love you, what benefit is that to you? For even sinners love those who love them. (Luke 6:32)

> For if you love those who love you, what reward do you have? Do not even tax collectors do the same? And if you greet only your brothers, what more are you doing than others? Do not even the Gentiles do the same? (Matt. 5:46-47)

Christ demands from his followers a supernatural, divine love that forgives, reconciles, and forebears—with the unlovely, with those who persecute us, hate us, with those outside our circle of church friends, with those who disagree with us, and with all people of the world. This is the love our heavenly Father displays, the love Jesus summons us to imitate.

---

36 Jonathan Edwards, "Religious Affections," ed. John E. Smith, in *The Works of Jonathan Edwards*, ed., Perry Miller (New Haven: Yale, 1959), 146.

Plan to Teach God's Principles of Love

Education is essential to nurturing love and changing people's attitudes and behavior. If you want your local church to be a loving, caring, Christlike church, then you must plan to teach the full spectrum of God's principles of love. If you want to cast a vision for your church to be a Christlike, loving community, speak of love often. Give warnings about the dangers of love that grows cold. Teach the truth of God's Word and give people principles of love to follow.

Someone or some group in the church needs to take the responsibility to plan for teaching biblical principles of love, or it will not happen. To make teaching on love a reality, one church devoted four summer months to teaching on love. They called the program "Summer of Love" and taught the major New Testament passages on love. They dedicated a full month to teaching 1 Corinthians 13:4-7. As individuals responded to the teaching of God's Word, the atmosphere of the church began to change. What a thrill it is to witness a revival of love within a church! May we be faithful to the example of Christ and the apostles and continue to teach the "more excellent way" of love (1 Cor. 12:31).

Chapter Four

Model Love

Our Lord was not an abstract theologian who sat in a classroom pontificating on the high virtues of love. Instead, Jesus "went about doing good" (Acts 10:38). He healed the sick, fed the multitudes, and preached the gospel to the poor. He exhausted himself in acts of kindness and deeds of compassion for the benefit of needy people. In every way, he lived and modeled a life of love. And after humbly and lovingly washing his disciples' feet, Jesus said, "For I have given you an example, that you also should do just as I have done to you" (John 13:15).

God has designed us in such a way that from infancy through adulthood we imitate other people (perhaps more than we would like to admit!). Since imitating others is a fundamental way in which we learn, it is important that we not only teach what the Bible says about love but that we model it. This is why the apostles modeled Christ's love and why Paul calls all believers to "be imitators of God" and live a life of love like his Son, Jesus Christ (Eph. 5:1-2).

> **"Be imitators of me, as I am of Christ."**

We encourage love in others by our example, and we learn the most about love when we see it lived out in the lives of people. Paul, for example, provided the church in Corinth with a much-needed example of Christlike love for them to see and imitate.[37] That is why—without any pride or boasting—he could urge the believers in Corinth to, "Be imitators of me, as I am of Christ" (1 Cor. 11:1). It is also why Paul commends Timothy for following his example of love (2 Tim. 3:10) and instructs him to be an example of love to others (1 Tim. 4:12).

---

[37] See also 1 Cor. 4:6, 16-17; 7:7; Gal. 4:12; Phil. 3:17; 4:9; 1 Thess. 1:6; 2 Thess. 3:6-9.

Knowing our need for good role models, God provides in his Word many inspiring examples from whom we can learn how to live a life of love. One of these examples is King David.

A Biblical Role Model of Love

When a newly elected president or prime minister takes office, the first statements or public acts become symbolic of the new administration's priorities and agenda. In one country, for example, a newly elected prime minister's first public statement was a promise to protect abortion rights, while in another country a new leader prayed for the nation. In one church, a pastor promised in his first Sunday morning sermon to hire the best youth pastor money can buy, while the pastor of another church preached his first sermon on the cross of Christ and led the congregation in celebrating the Lord's Supper. In each case, these new officials revealed their priorities and agenda by their first acts and public statements.

In the Old Testament, King David stands out as a role model of love for God. What was one of his first acts? Soon after he became king of Israel (2 Sam. 5:1-5), he built a dwelling place for the ark of God in Jerusalem.[38] David, along with tens of thousands of worshipers, priests, and Levites, celebrated as they moved the ark of God into Jerusalem. We read:

> So all Israel brought up the ark of the covenant of the LORD with shouting, to the sound of the horn, trumpets, and cymbals, and made loud music on harps and lyres.
>
> And David danced before the LORD with all his might.... (1 Chron. 15:27-28; 2 Sam. 6:13-14)

His initial act of moving the ark into Jerusalem demonstrated his highest priorities to be love for God, worship of God, and love of God's Law.

The ark of God was the most sacred object in Israel's worship. It symbolized the presence of the LORD (*YHWH*) God of Israel. For nearly a hundred years, the ark had been largely neglected. Saul, Israel's first king, neglected the ark of God and the nation's spiritual well-being (1 Chron. 13:3). But when David became king, he longed for the presence of God to be at the center of

---

[38] 2 Sam. 5:6-9; 6:1-15; 1 Chron. 13:1-6.

the nation and worship to be the nation's chief priority. So David wanted the ark to be kept in a permanent place in Jerusalem.

Not only did David bring the ark to Jerusalem, he filled the city with music and songs of praise. He reorganized the priests and Levites and put them all to work in the service and worship of the LORD. He appointed temple musicians and singers "to raise sounds of joy" (1 Chron. 15:16). The city literally was buzzing with the sounds of praise to God (1 Chron. 15-16). David's example of love for God brought spiritual reformation, revival, and renewal to Israel.

David also expressed his love in many poems and songs of worship to God. His praises are joyful and exuberant. His psalms are not just private musings; they are inspired by the Holy Spirit to help God's people worship him privately and publicly, in recitation and in song. David's life and psalms provide inspiration and enrichment that foster a deeper love for God.

Christian Biographies

In addition to following the examples of heroes of the faith in Scripture (Heb. 11), we can cultivate love by reading Christian biographies. A message of love for God and people is at the heart of Christian biographies. Thus a practical way to cultivate love is to read and share good Christian biographies with other people—especially with young people.

As a teenager, I worked at a summer Bible camp. While there, I was required to read certain biographies. The first two were about Hudson Taylor, founder of the China Inland Mission (now Overseas Missionary Fellowship), and George Müller, founder of the Ashley Down orphanage in Bristol, England.[39] Their complete devotion to God, passion for lost people, and sacrificial living exemplified by these two men remain in my mind today as a testimony of Christian love. Their example has not only been a powerful influence in my life, but in the lives of others. I have been amazed

---

[39] For an updated biography see Roger Steer, *George Müller: Delighted in God* (1975; reprint, ed., Fearn, Scotland: Christian Focus, 1997). Roger Steer, *J. Hudson Taylor: A Man in Christ* (Wheaton: Harold Shaw, 1993). Church historian Kenneth Scott Latourette writes, "Hudson Taylor was...one of the greatest missionaries of all time, and...one of the four or five most influential foreigners who came to China in the nineteenth century for any purpose..." (*A History of Christian Missions in China* [1929; reprint ed., New York: Russell & Russell, 1967], 382).

to discover how many prominent men and women of God have been trans-formed by reading the biographies of Müller and Taylor—people such as Amy Carmichael, Jim Elliot, Luis Palau, Billy and Ruth Graham, Francis and Edith Schaeffer.

Two additional biographies that have especially influenced my thinking about love are *L'Abri* and *Brother Indeed.*

L'Abri is the story of Francis and Edith Schaeffer who opened their home in the mountain village of Huemoz in the Swiss Alps to students and troubled people from all over the world who were seeking answers to the great philosophical and theological questions of life.[40] The Schaeffers had observed church communities fighting for orthodox doctrine but missing demonstrative love. So at *L'Abri* they sought to present biblical, historic Christian teaching within an observable, loving, Christian community. A major theme of the Schaeffers' life was costly, practical, observable love—the supernatural love of God lived out moment-by-moment in the daily lives of twentieth-century Christians.[41]

The other biography that has lifted my vision of love, *Brother Indeed*, is the story of Robert Chapman.[42] Chapman left his profession as a lawyer in London to become pastor of a small Baptist church in Barnstaple, England. This contentious little congregation had gone through three pastors in the eighteen months prior to his arrival. The story of how Chapman complete-ly turned around this fighting church by his love, patience, and Bible teach-ing is an inspiring account of loving leadership. By the end of his life, at age 99, Chapman had become so well known for his loving disposition and wis-dom that a letter from abroad addressed only to "R. C. Chapman, University of Love, England," was correctly delivered to his home. May our prayer be that our churches would become known as "Universities of Love."

---

40 Edith Schaeffer, *L'Abri* (Wheaton: Crossway, 1992).

41 Francis A. Schaeffer, *The Mark of the Christian* (Downers Grove: InterVarsity, 1970).

42 Frank Holmes, *Brother Indeed: The Life of Robert Cleaver Chapman* (London: Victory Press, 1956). For a more recent biography, see Robert L. Peterson, *Robert Chapman* (Littleton, CO: Lewis and Roth, 1995). For a short summary of Chapman's life and some of the remarkable ways he dealt with people, see Robert L. Peterson and Alexander Strauch, *Agape Leadership: Lessons in Spiritual Leadership from the Life of R.C. Chapman* (Littleton, CO: Lewis and Roth, 1991).

Local Church Leaders

Biographies are good, but people also need role models of love that they can see and hear in their own home and in their own church. One of the greatest needs in our churches today is for living examples of Christlike love. A church is blessed indeed if it has leaders who model love for God and love for people. Such leaders delight to worship and sing praises to God. They pray faithfully for the people, visit the sick, care for the needy, evangelize, teach God's Word, and sacrifice their time and money generously for the sake of others.

Church leaders set the tone for the church community. If local church leaders love, the people will love. If they are thoughtful, kind, and caring, the people will be thoughtful, kind, and caring. If they raise the awareness of people's needs and establish organizational structures through which people can serve needy members (Acts 6:1-7), the people will respond. If leaders create an environment of love and hold themselves and others accountable to love, the people will flourish spiritually and many will imitate their example. Even other churches may see and be spurred on to greater love (1 Thess. 1:7).

> *"There are many who preach Christ, but not many who live Christ. My great aim will be to live Christ."* —ROBERT CHAPMAN

Most Christians long for authentic, living, breathing examples of Christian love. When I asked one Christian woman who is known for her loving spirit and selfless service to others how she had learned to love, she told me it was by watching a body of loving church shepherds care for the congregation in which she was raised. You can be that example to those around you. You may not be a gifted preacher or scholar, but you can have a significant impact on people as you live and model Christlike love. You can be a change agent who initiates the growth of love in your church. "There are many who preach Christ," said Chapman, "but not many who live Christ. My great aim will be to *live* Christ."[43] This can be your aim in life also.

Parents

We experience the tenderness of love initially from our parents, so parents (and grandparents) have the greatest opportunities to teach and model God's love to impressionable children and adolescents. Our parents' love or lack of

---

[43] Peterson and Strauch, *Agape Leadership*, 14.

love has an enormous impact on our mental, emotional, and spiritual development. Studies have shown the tragic effects on children raised in orphanages where the children are left in cribs all day with little love, touch, affection, or interaction. These children develop lifelong physical, emotional, and mental problems.

In the same way that love matters to healthy human development, it also matters to healthy family and church development. If Christian parents love their children with Christlike love, they will, in most cases, produce children who are mentally, emotionally, and spiritually healthy. Paul, for example, reminds Timothy of the spiritual influence his grandmother Lois and mother Eunice had upon his faith and ministry (2 Tim 1:5; 3:15).[44]

If Christian parents love, serve, and reach out to people, they will, in most cases, produce children who love, serve, and reach out to help others. Many of the leaders and workers in churches today had parents who sacrificially loved and served God's people. These leaders and workers saw loving service modeled in their homes by their parents and have followed that example. A number of missionaries on the field today are products of missionary parents. In a few cases, fourth and fifth generation missionaries are serving today.[45]

If we want to teach and cultivate love in our churches, begin in the home, with your children and grandchildren. God wants you to be an example of his love to your family. People around you desperately need living examples of Christian love, and you can be that example. Love is the first fruit the Holy Spirit wants to produce and grow in your life (Gal. 5:22). Don't resist his gentle prodding; respond in obedience to the Spirit's leading to love as Christ loved. As Paul said to Timothy, "set the believers an example in…love" (1 Tim. 4:12).

---

[44] Deut. 4:9; 6:7, 20-25; Ps. 78:5-8; Ex. 10:2; 12:26-27; 13:8-10.

[45] For example, the Taylor family of China (Herbert H. Taylor, Maria Coulthard Taylor, J. H. Taylor II, J. H. Taylor III, J. H. Taylor IV); the Bell-Linton family of Korea (Eugene and Lottie Bell, Charlotte Bell Linton, Hugh Linton, and today Stephen, John, James, and Andrew Linton); and the Torrey family (R. A. Torrey, evangelist with D. L. Moody, R. A. Torrey II of China, R. A. Torrey III of Korea, and today Ben Torrey of Korea.).

Chapter Five

Guard Love

Cultivating love in the church must include the negative aspect of guarding against and warning about the dangers that threaten our love for God and our neighbor. We must love the right things in order to take preventative action to stop the loss of love. For example, John, the apostle, warns his readers, "Do not love the world or the things in the world. If anyone loves the world, the love of the Father is not in him" (1 John 2:15; also James 4:4; 2 Cor. 6:14-7:1).

When I think of what it means to guard our love, one image that comes to mind is of an advertisement for a wedding dress. The advertisement showed a beautiful bride looking down at her dress admiringly. The caption read, "Love him, but love your dress more." I think this captures a temptation we sometimes face in our love relationship with Christ. We love him, but do we love the material possessions and blessings he gives us more? Are we tempted to "love Christ, but love our home more?" To "love Christ, but love our money and securities more?" To "love Christ, but love our business more?" To "love Christ, but love our Christian ministry more?" Because of the ever-present temptation to love something else more than Christ, we must be ever vigilant to guard our love for Christ.

Every true believer loves Christ because not to love him means that one is not a believer. The Holy Spirit, who regenerates and indwells us, also moves us to love Christ. As believers, however, we can act selfishly and disobediently. We can let our love grow cold. Our love for Christ can be weakened by neglect, sin, worldly distractions, or false teaching (2 Cor. 11:2-4), so we must learn to guard it well.

Guard Your Love for Christ

In this world, which is hostile to Christ, plenty of contenders vie for our love. That is why the Bible says, "Keep yourselves in the love of God" (Jude 21).

That is why Jesus instructs the disciples to, "Abide in my love. If you keep my commandments, you will abide in my love, just as I have kept my Father's commandments and abide in his love" (John 15:9-10). Each of us must make a conscious effort at all times to guard our love relationship with Christ and to abide in his love through obedience to his Word.

> **"Abide in my love. If you keep my commandments, you will abide in my love."**
> JOHN 15:9-10

Mary of Bethany, the sister of Lazarus, is a biblical example of a believer who diligently guarded her love for Christ above all else. While Jesus was visiting in the home of his beloved friends Martha, Mary, and Lazarus, Luke tells us that Martha was "distracted with much serving," but Mary "sat at the Lord's feet and listened to his teaching" (Luke 10:39-40). Earlier, Mary no doubt had been in the kitchen working with Martha, but she left to spend time with Jesus and listen to his teaching. This caused Martha to complain, "Lord, do you not care that my sister has left me to serve alone? Tell her to help me" (Luke 10:40).

Both sisters loved Jesus, but Mary chose the course of action that would enrich her relationship with him. Martha did not. So in responding to Martha Jesus makes a clear distinction:

> Martha, Martha, you are anxious and troubled about many things, but *one thing is necessary*. Mary has chosen *the good portion*, which will not be taken away from her. (Luke 10:41-42; italics added)

Most of us are to some degree like Martha. We are easily distracted by our work. We become anxious about the many details of life and neglect spending time with Christ. Martha loved Jesus but became so preoccupied with her work *for* the Lord that she didn't have time to enjoy being *with* him, which was the very thing Jesus would have preferred. Her well-meaning service for Christ actually dragged her away from his presence. Instead of joy, she experienced anger and frustration—and not just toward Mary but also toward him.

Mary, on the other hand, knew when to set other things aside and spend time with her Lord. She put Christ first and her work second. She chose to stop everything else, listen to his words, and cultivate her love for him.

How important it is for us to remember this succinct statement of Jesus:

One thing is necessary.

When we read and study God's Word, it is as if we are sitting at Jesus' feet and listening to his wonderful teachings. Jesus himself tells us that the whole of the Scriptures speak of him. He is its grand theme.[46] We can't love him if we don't know him, and we learn to know him by the Scriptures that reveal him to us. We simply cannot guard our love nor can we grow in our love for Christ without spending time regularly in his Word. So the question is: What is distracting you from spending time at Jesus' feet and listening to his words?

It is easy to become so busy that we have no time for God and no time for the Word and prayer. The director of a world mission organization recognizes this risk and has on his desk a sign that reads, "Beware of the barrenness of a busy life." The right balance is difficult to achieve, but we must recognize the danger of being "distracted with much serving" (Luke 10:40).

> **We can't love him if we don't know him, and we learn to know him by the Scriptures that reveal him to us.**

It is also easy to be distracted from loving God because of our love for sports, material prosperity, career advancement, television, or movies. When any of these things govern our life and demand our heart, soul, and strength, they steal our time away from Christ. These things can become modern idols and heavy burdens that slow us down and prevent us from running the race that is set before us (Heb. 12:1-2). Good things can become bad things when they siphon our time or divert our affection away from Christ. To guard our love, may the prayer of that godly saint, Samuel Rutherford, become our own: "I am most gladly content that Christ breaketh all my idols in pieces: it hath put a new edge upon my blunted love to Christ."[47]

> **Beware of the barrenness of a busy life.**

Not one of us is exempt from the temptation of becoming careless about our love for Christ. In Paul's last letter to Timothy, he writes that Demas, a co-worker in the gospel, deserted him because he loved "this present world" (2 Tim. 4:10). Love for the world's possessions and comforts turned Demas's heart away from serving Christ and suffering for the gospel. Demas did not abide in Christ's love (John 15:9-10); he did not guard his love for Christ.

---

[46] John 5:39, 46; Luke 24:27, 44; see also Deut. 8:3.

[47] Samuel Rutherford, *The Loveliness of Christ: Extracts from the Letters of Samuel Rutherford* (1909; reprint ed., Edinburgh: Banner of Truth, 2008), 86.

David Gooding, former professor of Greek at Queens College in Belfast, Ireland, reminds us that we must make a deliberate, conscious choice to choose the "good portion" in life which will never be taken away from us:

> We cannot do everything: there is not enough time. Like Mary, therefore, we shall have to choose and choose very deliberately. Life's affairs will not automatically sort themselves into a true order of priorities. If we do not consciously insist on making 'sitting at the Lord's feet and listening to his word' our number one necessity, a thousand and one other things and duties, all claiming to be prior necessities, will tyrannize our time and energies and rob us of the 'good part' in life.[48]

We can make this choice only after we order life according to the correct priority. In his classic devotional, *My Utmost for His Highest*, Oswald Chambers sets before us the only correct priority to guide and guard us:

> Jesus taught that a disciple has to make his relationship to God the dominating concentration of his life, and to be carefully careless about everything else in comparison to that.[49]

Guard Your Love for Others

If we must jealously guard our love for Christ, we need also to guard our love for people. Just as the Holy Spirit moves us to love Christ, he motivates us to sacrificially love others. But as we have seen, believers can act selfishly and disobey God's Word. As the eighteenth-century evangelist Henry Moorhouse observed in a letter to a friend, "Love seems in so many hearts to have gone to sleep."[50]

"Love seems in so many hearts to have gone to sleep."
—HENRY MOORHOUSE

---

48 David Gooding, *According to Luke: A New Exposition of the Third Gospel* (Grand Rapids: Eerdmans, 1987), 216.

49 Oswald Chambers, *My Utmost for His Highest* (New York: Dodd, Mead & Company, 1935), 142 (the selection for May 21).

50 Macpherson, Henry Moorhouse, 117.

"A new commandment...
love one another:
just as I have loved you."
(John 13:34)

When love goes to sleep, we grow cold and unfeeling toward people. We love material possessions and personal comforts more than people. We love our work more than people. We become bitter toward people because our feelings have been hurt. We become weary in serving selfish, ungrateful people and become content to show love only to those who are agreeable to us. We become lazy and complacent about love. We neglect our duty to love the unlovely and the disagreeable. Like the priest and Levite in the story of the Good Samaritan, we become apathetic to the suffering of others.

Even though we know that "love is the jewel among the graces of the Christian life,"[51] it is so easy to neglect our duty and forsake loving others as Christ loved. Maurice Roberts captures the disparity between what we know of love and how we live out its demands in our lives:

> We see the very incarnation of God's love in the Gospel-portrait of Christ. We behold him as he first washes the disciples' feet and then mounts the cross to wash their souls. But hardly has the memory of this transcendent love faded from our thoughts than we find ourselves reverting to our old habits of self-seeking and self-interest. No marvel the prophet exclaimed, "Woe is me! [Isa. 6:5] and the apostle, "O wretched man that I am!" [Rom. 7:24].[52]

So when you sense your love falling to sleep, take corrective action immediately. The longer you wait, the harder it will be to awaken the spirit of love. Turn to the Scriptures and let them revive your sleepy soul. Pray for a fresh awakening of gratitude for the free grace of God and for the costly sacrifice of Christ at Calvary's cross.[53] Pray earnestly that the Lord would fill you anew with the first fruit of the Spirit which is love (Gal. 5:22; Eph. 5:18). Repent of any sin that dulls your love for God or his people. Stop thinking about yourself so much. Follow the great examples of those who have modeled the life

---

51 Roberts, "The Supreme Grace of Christian Love," 4.

52 Roberts, "The Supreme Grace of Christian Love," 4.

53 Jerry Bridges provides sound biblical advice for maintaining love and holiness when he says we should preach the gospel to ourselves every day (*The Discipline of Grace: God's Role and Our Role in the Pursuit of Holiness* [Colorado Springs: NavPress, 1994], 45-60; *The Gospel for Real Life: Turn to the Liberating Power of the Cross...Every Day* [Colorado Springs: NavPress, 2003]).

of love God desires. Remind yourself of your first Christian duty to love God and neighbor. Start doing outward acts of love for others and pray that soon the desire and joy of loving others will follow.

For those who have drifted far from the Christian spirit of love, Jesus says to wake up, remember from where you have fallen, repent of your sin, and do the deeds of love you once did (Rev. 2:5). In order to avoid becoming like the Ephesian Christians who needed to repent of their loss of love, heed the practical advice of Jonathan Edwards:

> *"A Christian should at all times keep a strong guard against everything that tends to overthrow or corrupt or undermine a spirit of love."*
> —JONATHAN EDWARDS

> A Christian should at all times keep a strong guard against everything that tends to overthrow or corrupt or undermine a spirit of love. That which hinders love to men, will hinder the exercise of love to God…. If love is the sum of Christianity, surely those things which overthrow love are exceedingly unbecoming [to] Christians.[54]

Don't let your love go to sleep, be spiritually awake. "Keep yourselves in the love of God" (Jude 21). At "all times keep a strong guard against everything that tends to overthrow or corrupt or undermine a spirit of love."

---

[54] Jonathan Edwards, *Charity and Its Fruits*, 23.

Chapter Six

Practice Love

Studying love is exciting, being taught the doctrines of love is enlightening, praying about love is heart moving, and seeing love modeled is motivating, but in the end, we must lovingly obey God and sacrificially serve people. We must be practitioners of love, not theorists. We must be doers of love, not talkers. We must forge a connection between words and actions.

Knowing how easy it is to talk the talk of love but not walk the walk of love, the apostle John warns,

> But if anyone has the world's goods and sees his brother in need, yet closes his heart against him, how does God's love abide in him? Little children, let us *not love in word or talk but in deed and in truth.* (1 John 3:16; italics added)

Paul also exhorted his readers to practice genuine love: "Let love be genuine" (Rom. 12:9). After stating his theme of sincere, genuine love, he proceeds to list many acts and attitudes of sincere, genuine love (Rom. 12:9-21). He expects his readers to obey these instructions, not just talk of their virtuous qualities.

And James would warn of the danger of being a mere hearer or admirer of love, rather than "a doer who acts" in love (James 1:22-25). Only the one who acts is blessed, not the one who sits in church and hears but immediately forgets. James would also remind us that love "apart from works is dead" (James 2:26).

Because it is so easy to talk the language of love without living the reality of love, the apostles had to continually remind and exhort believers to practice the love they professed. We must do the same today. We must practice Christlike love ourselves and exhort one another to practice love.

Divine love bears practical fruit (Gal. 5:22). It prompts sacrificial service

(Gal. 5:13), acts of kindness (1 Cor. 13:4), and strenuous labor on the behalf of the needs of others (1 Thess. 1:3). "A true *love* for people," says John Stott, "leads to labour for them; otherwise it degenerates into mere sentimentality."[55] To refuse to practice love "in deed and in truth" would be to disobey Christ's commands to love God, our neighbor, our fellow believers, our enemies, and all people. We must remember that the biblical commands to love require obedience and practical action on our part. They are not heavenly suggestions, but direct commands from the King.

Obedience to Christ's commands to love leads to real growth in love.

In Scripture, love and obedience are inseparable companions.[56] Obedience to Christ's commands to love leads to real growth in love. Disobedience leads to an erosion of love. Thus cultivating an atmosphere of love in the church is inescapably connected to cultivating an atmosphere of obedience to God's Word and Spirit. "Love is not," as biblical commentator Alexander Ross explains, "an emotion to which we may give expression now and then, as we feel inclined; it is a duty required of us at all times by God, and the children of God ought surely to obey their Heavenly Father."[57]

Since love "is a duty required of us at all times by God," *we need to commit ourselves afresh to the obedient practice of Christ's principles of love.* Just as marriage is a commitment to love one another in good times and in bad, so love for God and neighbor is a commitment to love God and neighbor despite changing feelings or difficult circumstances. If you want to love as Christ loved, com-

---

55 John R. W. Stott, *The Message of Thessalonians: The Gospel & the End of Time*, BST (Downers Grove: InterVarsity, 1991), 30. Commenting on the phrase "labor of love" in 1 Thessalonians 1:3, James Denny calls *"laboriousness"* "love's characteristic" (*The Epistles to the Thessalonians,* The Expositor's Bible [New York: Eaton & Mains, n. d.], 29). Of Paul's example of labor, Denny writes, "Love set [Paul], and will set every one in whose heart it truly burns, *upon incessant, unwearied efforts for others' good.* Paul was ready to spend and be spent at its bidding, however small the result might be. He toiled with his hands, he toiled with his brain, he toiled with his ardent, eager, passionate heart, he toiled in his continual intercessions with God, and all these toils made up his labour of love" (p 28, italics added).

56 Ex. 20:6; Deut. 10:12-13; 11:1, 13, 22; 19:9; 30:16, 19-20; John 14:15, 21, 31; 15:10; 1 John 2:5; 5:3; 2 John 6.

57 Alexander Ross, *The Epistles of James and John,* NICNT (Grand Rapids: Eerdmans, 1954), 208.

mit yourself to love as he loved (Eph. 5:2; 1 John 3:16). If you want to pursue love, commit yourself to the pursuit of biblical love (1 Cor. 14:1). If you want to do all things in love, commit yourself to doing everything in love (1 Cor. 16:14). If you want to stir up love in the church, commit yourself to thinking and acting in ways that inspire love in others (Heb. 10:24).

Nearly forty-five years ago, Herb and Alice Banks, along with other families, founded our present church. For years they have selflessly served the people of our church. Their labors are legendary. They visited the sick in hospitals, prisoners in jail, seniors in nursing homes, and missionaries on the field. They taught Bible studies and led our missions program. For thirty-eight years, Herb served as one of our pastor elders. In the past, nearly everyone in the church had been to their home to enjoy their gracious hospitality. Only now, due to ill health, has their service waned. To their way of thinking, however, Herb and Alice didn't do anything special. They simply did what the Lord commanded: "love one another as I have loved you" (John 13:34-35). They translated biblical convictions into action. Their love for the Lord and obedience to his Word motivated and sustained their loving service for people until they were well into their eighties.

Although Christ commands us to love as he loved, he doesn't leave us powerless to accomplish the task. He graciously gives his life-empowering Holy Spirit. The Holy Spirit—who is God and is love—produces within every believer a supernatural capacity to love as Christ loves.[58] In the words of biblical commentator R. S. Candlish, "We have now a divine faculty of loving; we love with the love which is of God; which is God's very nature."[59] The first fruit the Holy Spirit produces in the believer's life is "love" (Gal. 5:22).

The love of God that has been "poured into our hearts through the Holy Spirit" (Rom 5:5) motivates us to love and obey with joy the commands of love. Indeed, we obey his commandments because we love him. "If you love me," Jesus says, "you will keep my commandments" (John 14:15). Jesus is speaking of loving, willing obedience from the heart, not a forced or joyless obedience. We also delight in obedience because of our gratitude for his love and sacrifice for us. He has rescued us "from the

---

[58] Rom. 5:5; 15:30; Gal. 5:22; also Deut. 30:6.
[59] R. S. Candlish, *The First Epistle of John,* 2d ed. (1869; reprint ed., Grand Rapids: Zondervan, n.d.), 422, 423

domain of darkness" (Col. 1:13), from sin and death, and given us eternal life. What can we do in response to such love, but to love and obey?

After his resurrection, Jesus confronted Peter, who had denied him three times. On the shore of the Sea of Galilee, Jesus asked Peter three times, "do you love me?" (John 21:15-17).

Each time Peter affirmed his love for Christ: "Yes, Lord; you know that I love you."

After each of Peter's public confessions of love, Jesus responded by charging Peter to care for his people: "Feed my lambs...tend my sheep...feed my sheep."

The proof of Peter's profession of love and the reality of his love would be found in his practical obedience to Christ's command to shepherd Christ's people. As the book of Acts happily reports, Peter, enabled by the Holy Spirit, proved his profession of love for Christ by a life dedicated to caring for Christ's flock. May our public profession of love for God and neighbor also be backed by the genuine practice of Christian love (Rom. 12:9-21).

Restored Love

Perhaps you are wondering how the church in Ephesus responded when Christ's letter was read publicly in the assembly. Did they humble themselves before God? Did they obey the Lord's directives? Or did they refuse to believe the Lord's assessment of their spiritual condition?

We find the answer in a letter written at the beginning of the second century by Ignatius, the overseer (Greek, *episcopos*) of the church at Antioch in Syria. Ignatius had been arrested for his faith and was sent by Roman guard to Rome for execution some time between A.D. 105-117. While on his journey to Rome, Ignatius wrote seven letters that remain to this day. These letters are traditionally placed among other documents known as the writings of the Apostolic Fathers. One of those letters was written to the church at Ephesus.

On the way to Rome, Ignatius's guards stopped in the city of Smyrna. While at Smyrna, the church in Ephesus, about forty miles south, sent a delegation of brothers to encourage and strengthen Ignatius as he faced martyrdom in Rome. So uplifting was their visit that Ignatius wrote a letter thanking them for their thoughtfulness and care. In this letter he praises their love, commending them as a church "characterized by faith in and love of Christ

Jesus our Savior."[60] He rejoices that they "love nothing in human life, only God."[61] He also comments on their church overseer, Onesimus, calling him "a man of inexpressible love."[62] Ignatius goes on to write that in the Ephesian representatives who visited him in Smyrna he could see the love of the whole church in Ephesus.[63]

Thus, at the beginning of the second century, we know that the church in Ephesus was very much alive. It was sound in doctrine and abounding in love. The Ephesian believers had obeyed the Lord's call to remember, repent, and do their first works. As a result, the church's love was restored. "He who has an ear," declares the Lord, "let him hear what the Spirit says to the churches" (Rev. 2:7).

---

[60] Ignatius, *To the Ephesians,* 1.2 in *The Apostolic Fathers,* 3rd edition, Michael W. Holmes (Grand Rapids: Baker, 2007).

[61] Ignatius, *To the Ephesians,* 9.2.

[62] Ignatius, *To the Ephesians,* 1.3.

[63] Ignatius, *To the Ephesians,* 2.1.

Part Three

STUDY GUIDE

Do your best to present yourself to God as one approved,
a worker who has no need to be ashamed, rightly handling the word of truth.
2 Tim. 2:15

Lesson One:

The Problem of Lost Love, Christ's Commendation and Complaint, and When a Church Loses Its Love

(For the discussion leader, answers to the following questions are provided on the download page at www.lewisandroth.org)

1. In Revelation chapters two and three, Christ gives his evaluation of the seven churches in Asia Minor. List two reasons why Christ's evaluation of these churches should matter to us today.

2. In your own words, briefly list the commendable qualities of the church in Ephesus that Christ praises. Of all the positive traits you listed, which one do you think was the church's most commendable quality? Explain.

3. Despite all the church's commendable qualities, something was dreadfully wrong in the church at Ephesus. In your own words, clearly describe the problem. Be as specific as possible.

4. The church in Ephesus "abandoned" its first love. What factors do you think may have caused this otherwise good church to forsake its original condition of love?

5. How have the six points about the importance of love changed your way of thinking about love? Which point impacted you most deeply? Explain.

6. Why is the doctrine of the Trinity foundational to the Christian doctrine of love? List as many reasons as you can. (See footnote 10, page 16.)

7. What does the author mean by the statement, "the sum of all God's commandments and all religious service is love for God"? Is there a Scripture passage to back up this statement?

8. What does Luke 10:25-37 teach you about the meaning of loving "your neighbor as yourself"? List at least two principles taught by this passage.

9. In light of the Old Testament commandments to love God and neighbor (Deut. 6:4-5; Lev. 19:18), what is "new" about the "new commandment" of Jesus (John 13:34-35)?

10. First Corinthians 13:1-3 is considered to be one of Paul's most skillfully written passages. What is the main point of this literary masterpiece?

11. Make two columns on a sheet of paper. On the left, list wrong attitudes that ruin the Christian spirit or atmosphere of a local church. On the right, list as many correct biblical attitudes and qualities as you can. If you can, list Scripture to support your answers.

Wrong attitudes and qualities	Correct biblical attitudes and qualities

   a. Why is it important that a local church have a proper New Testament church atmosphere? List at least two reasons.

   b. Why are prideful attitudes about correct knowledge and denominational distinctions so destructive to the spirit of a local church?

12. Below is a list of ways to help develop and maintain a deeper love relationship with God through Jesus Christ. Carefully read these statements and answer the questions at the end.

   (1) by a personal commitment (with the Holy Spirit's help) to obey "the great and first commandment" to love God unreservedly and to love the Lord Jesus Christ preeminently above all others. Deut. 6:4-5; 13:3; Jos. 23:11; Ps. 27:4; Matt. 10:37; 22:37-38; Mark 12:28-34; Luke 10:25-28; 14:26; John 21:15-17; Phil. 1:21; 3:13-14).

(2) by reading, studying, and meditating on God's Word, the Scriptures, in order to know Him as the great God that He is (Deut. 17:18-20). D. A. Carson doesn't hesitate to say,

> but I doubt that it is possible to obey the first command without reading the Bible a great deal....
>
> How on earth shall we love him with heart and mind if we do not increasingly know him, know what he likes and what he loathes, know what he has disclosed, know what he commands and what he forbids (D. A. Carson, *Love in Hard Places* [Wheaton: Crossway, 2002], 32)?

(3) by communing regularly with Him in prayer: "Be constant in prayer" (Rom.12:12). This will include confession of sin, praise, and intercession for others.

(4) by living in obedience to Christ's commands: "For this is the love of God [love for God], that we keep his commandments" (1 John 5:3).

(5) by not loving the world and its idols: "Do not love the world or the things in the world. If anyone loves the world, the love of the Father [love for the Father] is not in him" (1 John 2:15; also James 4:4).

(6) by loving and serving God's people: "For he who does not love his brother whom he has seen cannot love God whom he has not seen. And this commandment we have from him: whoever loves God must also love his brother" (1 John 4:20-21; also 4:11-12, 20; James 1:27).

(7) by worshiping him in song, praise, thanksgiving, and "in remembrance" of his substitutionary death through the elements of the bread and cup (1 Cor. 11:23-32; Rev. 5:9-14).

    a. Of these seven ways to deepen your love relationship with God through Christ, which two are the most difficult for you to practice consistently? Explain why.

    b. Of these seven ways to deepen your love relationship with God through Christ, which two help you most to maintain your relationship with Christ? Explain.

c. Of these seven ways to deepen your love relationship with God through Christ, which one needs your immediate attention? Describe several steps you can take to improve.

Christ's Remedy and Study Love

1. The author states, "External religious performance can insidiously replace true, inner faith and heartfelt love." Give an example (preferably from your own church experience) of what the author means by this statement. For help, see Luke 11:42 and Matt. 23:23-28.

2. In what way is Revelation 2:4 a vitally important wake-up call to all churches?

3. Why is it difficult to restore lost love to a local church? List as many reasons as you can.

4. Jesus commands the Ephesians to "remember therefore from where you have fallen" (Rev. 2:5). What is the purpose of remembering from where they had fallen? What good would it do?

5. On pages 21-22 the author lists five bullet points explaining what repentance would entail for the church in Ephesus. Read each of these five points and make a brief note on the meaning of each one in order to be prepared to discuss each point with your study group. As a group, discuss each point so that every member understands clearly what is involved for a church to repent of lost love. This exercise will help you to grasp the full meaning of the New Testament word repentance. Also, reread D. A. Carson's definition of repentance.

6. What do you think were some of the "first works" of love that needed to be revived? List as many works as you can and be as specific as you can be. Be creative in your answer.

7. In Part Two of the book, the author lists six suggestions on how to cultivate love. Why did the author start with the study of love?

8. According to each of the verses below, what responsibilities do we have in regard to cultivating love? Feel free to use Bible commentaries about the following verses to help you answer the questions.

> John 15:9-10
> 1 Corinthians 14:1
> Ephesians 5:1-2
> Hebrews 10:24
> Jude 21

9. Why do we need the Bible to understand love? List as many reasons as you can.

10. Read the biblical passages on love in Appendix B and answer the following questions.

> **a.** Which Old Testament text most spoke to you about God's amazing love for his people?
>
> **b.** In your estimation, which Old Testament text best reveals that God is Love?
>
> **c.** What does Romans 13:8 teach you about your obligation to love?
>
> **d.** Which New Testament texts most comfort your heart when facing difficult trials and tragedies? Explain your answer.
>
> **e.** Which one New Testament text from the list would you choose for a life verse if you were asked to choose one? Explain your choice.

11. How would you go about encouraging another believer (church member, family member, friend, or missionary) to start studying biblical love?

Lesson Three:

Pray for Love and Teach Love

1. Why is it necessary to pray about growth in Christlike love? List as many reasons as you can.

2. Before answering this question, have someone read Ephesians 3:14-19 to your group. Why does the author emphasize the extreme importance of understanding Ephesians 3:18-19 in order to grow in love?

3. List as many reasons as you can why Christians should never stop growing in their love.

4. Maurice Roberts writes, "the best believers find their progress [in love] slow and their attainments meager." Why is it difficult to grow in our love for God and neighbor?

5. The author says, "These Spirit-inspired prayers [1 Thess. 3:12; Phil. 1:9; Jude 2] are wonderful models to pray for ourselves and for others." How would you put these scriptural prayers into your own words in order to pray for yourself, your family, your local church, and your missionaries? How would you put Ephesians 3:18-19 in your own words in order to pray this prayer for yourself?

6. After reading the fifteen descriptions of love found in 1 Corinthians 13:4-7, which two of the negative statements about love do you think are most destructive to relationships within a local church? Explain your choices.

7. Which two of the fifteen qualities of love do you need to be most concerned about in order to improve your love and character? Explain your choices.

8. Why do you think family relationships at home provide the best testing ground for the practice of Christlike love? List at least three reasons.

9. In order to cultivate love, it is vital that you understand Hebrews 10:24-25. Look up these verses in your Bible and answer the following questions.

   a. What does the word "consider" mean? What are some English synonyms? To help, use Bible commentaries or a dictionary.

   b. What does the phrase "stir up" mean? What are some English synonyms?

   c. Who is to do the "considering" and "stirring up"?

   d. Why does neglecting to meet regularly with the church family hinder growth in love?

   e. In what ways is life together in the local church a means of testing and building Christlike love?

   f. List one practical way you can stir up another person to grow in love.

10. List a few key Scripture passages that show that every single member in the local church, not just the leaders, is responsible for building up the church in love. (For a list of Scripture texts, see footnotes 32 through 34, page 47.) Which one passage is most convincing to you? Explain why.

11. Explain how Christian love is different from the natural, human love which all people feel for friends and relatives. Why is it critically important to understand this difference?

12. In order to change a church's attitudes, behaviors, and works, why is it necessary to teach the Scriptures on God's principles of love?

Lesson Four:

Model Love and Guard Love

1. Why did Paul feel so strongly about the need to model the Christian life for his new converts? (For help, see 1 Cor. 4:16-17; 11:1; Phil. 3:1-18; 2 Thess. 3:7-10.)

2. King David is a biblical role model of love for God. What specifically did David do that demonstrated his total love for God? List several of David's acts of love for God.

3. What did David do that you can also do to show the priority of love for God in your life and ministry? Be specific and practical in your answers.

4. Why are biographies of Christians helpful in challenging people to grow in love? Have you read a Christian biography that has challenged you to grow in love? If so, share this with your group.

5. Why is it important for church leaders to model love? List several reasons.

6. What are some specific things church leaders can do to influence the atmosphere of the church to grow in love?

7. How can you, whether you are in a position of leadership or not, influence the atmosphere of love in your church? Be specific.

8. Why can parents and grandparents, more than anyone else, influence their children to become lovers of God and people?

9. Jesus told his disciples to "abide in my love" (John 15:9-10). Practically, how do we abide in Christ's love? Be sure to read the passage in John before answering the question.

10. Before answering the next few questions, have someone read Luke 10:38-42 to your group. In what ways are we all like Martha?

11. What is the "one thing" that Jesus says is necessary in life? What is the "good portion" which Jesus says will not be taken away from Mary?

12. How did Mary show her love for Christ? List as many things as you can.

13. What practical steps can you take to fight the "Martha syndrome" (over-busyness and wrong priorities)?

Guard Love and Practice Love

1. Name some of the hostile enemies to your love relationship with Jesus Christ that you must be aware of at all times. Can you think of any Scripture passages that help you identify these love killers?

2. What practical steps can you take to guard your love relationship with Christ? Of the steps you listed, which one step is most important to you personally?

3. What does Oswald Chambers mean when he says that we should be "carefully careless about everything else"?

4. What most discourages you from loving people as you should? What can you do about the problem?

5. If you sense your love for people growing cold, what actions can you take to fan the flame of neighborly love?

6. What does Jerry Bridges mean by "preaching the gospel to yourself every day"? How could you benefit from preaching the gospel to yourself every day? (See footnote 53.)

7. What problems do we create in the local church if we only talk about love without practicing the biblical commands of love? List as many problems as you can.

8. What does James Denny mean by calling laboriousness "love's characteristic"? (See footnote 55)

9. Before answering this question, have someone read Romans 12:9-21 to your group. Using Romans 12:9-21, list five acts or attitudes of sincere, genuine love. What two are most needed in order to help your church become a more loving, caring community?

10. What does Alexander Ross mean by the statement, "Love is not an emotion to which we may give expression now and then, as we feel inclined"?

11. Explain how obedience to Christ's commands of love leads to real growth in love. Explain how disobedience to Christ's commands of love leads to an erosion of love.

12. Explain briefly each verse below and find the common idea in each verse that makes obedience to Christ's love commands possible.

       Romans 5:5
       Romans 15:30
       Galatians 5:22

13. What would you say to a person who uses this book (*Love or Die*) to criticize and accuse other believers of not having any love?

Appendix A:
Other Books on Love
by Alexander Strauch

Reading books on biblical love will help build loving Christian community and develop loving leaders. It is recommended that the books listed below be considered as a unit and read in the following order:

Love or Die: Christ's Wake-Up Call to the Church, Revelation 2:4. This book is an exposition of Revelation 2:4, a vitally important passage to every local church and its leaders. It also presents practical ways to cultivate love individually but especially in the local church family.

Agape Leadership: Lessons in Spiritual Leadership from the Life of R. C. Chapman was written to provide a model of the kind of radical love the New Testament envisions for Christians to emulate. This small eighty-page booklet features examples of how Robert Chapman handled difficult life situations according to biblical principles of love. (For a full biography of Chapman's life, read *Robert Chapman: A Biography* by Robert L. Peterson.)

A Christian Leader's Guide to Leading With Love presents and applies the biblical principles of love to anyone leading or caring for people. A study guide is also available.

The Hospitality Commands: Building Loving Christian Community, Building Bridges to Friends and Neighbors. Hospitality is one of the most powerful ways to build loving Christian community, and it is one of the biblical love commands. This book is closely connected with *Leading with Love*. Study guide included.

Ministers of Mercy: The New Testament Deacon is a book to help deacons understand their official role in the church as ministers of benevolence, mercy, and loving care for needy members. A loving church community takes very seriously the care for its needy, vulnerable members. Reading this book may inspire you to want to be a deacon. A study guide is also available.

Appendix B:

Fifty Key Texts on Love

Read and slowly meditate on each of these fifty texts of Scripture. If you desire, look up each text in your Bible so that you can read each one in its full context. Don't rush! Say with the Psalmist "O how I love Your law! It is my meditation all the day" (Ps. 119:97).

1. The Lord...proclaimed, "The Lord, the Lord, a God merciful and gracious...abounding in steadfast love." (Ex. 34:6)
2. You shall love your neighbor as yourself. (Lev. 19:18)
3. You shall love the Lord your God with all your heart and with all your soul and with all your might. (Deut. 6:5)
4. It was not because you were more in number than any other people that the Lord set his love on you and chose you...but it is because the Lord loves you and is keeping the oath that he swore to your fathers. (Deut. 7:7-8)
5. Yet the Lord set his heart in love on your fathers and chose their offspring after them. (Deut. 10:15)
6. But I have trusted in your steadfast love. (Ps. 13:5)
7. His steadfast love endures forever. (Ps. 106:1)
8. In his love and in his pity he redeemed them. (Isa. 63:9)
9. I have loved you with an everlasting love; therefore I have continued my faithfulness to you. (Jer. 31:3)
10. And the Lord said to me [Hosea], "Go again, love a woman [Gomer] who is loved by another man and is an adulteress, even as the Lord loves the children of Israel, though they turn to other gods." (Hosea 3:1)
11. I will love them [Israel] freely. (Hosea 14:4)
12. Love your enemies. (Matt. 5:43)
13. You shall love the Lord your God with all your heart.... This is the great and first commandment. And a second is like it: You shall love your neighbor as yourself. On these two commandments depend all the Law and the Prophets. (Matt. 22:37-40)

14. For God so loved the world, that he gave his only Son. (John 3:16)

15. The Father loves the Son. (John 3:35)

16. If you love me, you will keep my commandments. (John 14:15)

17. I [the Son] love the Father. (John 14:31)

18. If you keep my commandments, you will abide in my love, just as I have kept my Father's commandments and abide in his love. (John 15:10)

19. As the Father has loved me, so have I loved you. Abide in my love. (John 15:9)

20. Who shall separate us from the love of Christ?... [Nothing] in all creation, will be able to separate us from the love of God in Christ Jesus our Lord. (Rom. 8:35, 39)

21. Let love be genuine. (Rom. 12:9)

22. Owe no one anything, except to love each other. (Rom. 13:8)

23. Love is the fulfilling of the law. (Rom. 13:10)

24. Knowledge puffs up, but love builds. (1 Cor. 8:1)

25. And I will show you a still more excellent way [love]. (1 Cor. 12:31)

26. If I...understand all mysteries and all knowledge...but have not love, I am nothing. (1 Cor. 13:2)

27. The greatest of these is love. (1 Cor. 13:13)

28. Pursue love. (1 Cor. 14:1)

29. Let all that you do be done in love. (1 Cor. 16:14)

30. For the love of Christ controls us. (2 Cor. 5:14)

31. The fruit of the Spirit is love. (Gal. 5:22)

32. But God...because of the great love with which he loved us...made us alive together with Christ. (Eph. 2:4)

33. To know the love of Christ that surpasses knowledge. (Eph. 3:19)

34. Walk in love, as Christ loved us and gave himself up for us. (Eph. 5:2)

35. And this is my prayer that your love may abound more and more. (Phil. 1:9)

36. And above all these put on love, which binds everything together in perfect harmony. (Col. 3:14)

37. May the Lord make you increase and abound in love for one another and for all. (1 Thess. 3:12)

38. The aim of our charge is love. (1 Tim. 1:5)

39. And let us consider how to stir up one another to love. (Heb. 10:24)

40. Love one another earnestly from a pure heart. (1 Peter 1:22)

41. Above all, keep loving one another earnestly, since love covers a multitude of sins. (1 Peter 4:8)

42. Whoever does not love abides in death. (1 John 3:14)

43. By this we know love, that he laid down his life for us. (1 John 3:16)

44. Let us not love in word or talk but in deed and in truth. (1 John 3:18)

45. Beloved, let us love one another, for love is from God, and whoever loves has been born of God and knows God. (1 John 4:7)

46. God is love. (1 John 4:8)

47. In this is love, not that we have loved God but that he loved us and sent his Son to be the propitiation for our sins. (1 John 4:10)

48. We love because he first loved us. (1 John 4:19)

49. Keep yourselves in the love of God. (Jude 21)

50. To him [Jesus] who loves us and has freed us from our sins by his blood. (Rev. 1:5)

General Index of Names

Scripture Index

About the Author

For the past forty years Alexander Strauch has served as a teaching elder at the Littleton Bible Chapel in Littleton, Colorado. Additionally, he has taught philosophy and New Testament literature at Colorado Christian University. A gifted Bible teacher and popular speaker, Alexander Strauch has helped thousands of churches worldwide through his expository writing and preaching ministry. He is the author of more than a dozen books, including *Biblical Eldership,* which has sold over 250,000 copies. Alexander Strauch's books have been translated into more than twenty languages.

Alexander and his wife Marilyn reside in Littleton, Colorado, near their four adult daughters and eight grandchildren.

For more details about Alexander Strauch and his books and audio messages, contact Lewis and Roth Publishers at 800-477-3239 or www.lewisandroth.org. If you are calling from outside the United States, please call 719-494-1800.

Acknowledgments

Many friends have contributed to the completion of this book, friends who love the Lord and his people.

I want to acknowledge Douglas VanSchooneveld for his helpful suggestions and for his time spent checking sources, verifying quotations, and documenting footnotes. His passion for the subject of Christian love exceeds my own.

I offer special thanks to my editors Amanda Sorenson and Shannon Wingrove. They are a joy to work with and their creative recommendations are greatly appreciated. Thanks also to Paul and Laura Lundgren for typing and offering helpful suggestions.

Also, I would like to thank Barbara Peek, who proofread the final manuscript; Jani Bennett, who typeset the book; David MacLeod, who checked the footnotes; and Jay Brady, who helped me with many practical matters.

I gratefully acknowledge the time and effort Danny and Paola Pasquale devoted to working through all the study questions while on furlough from their work in Italy.

And, as always, I would like to express special appreciation to Marilyn, my loving wife and chief helper in life and ministry.

To all my precious friends, fellow workers, and those who read this book, "May grace be with all those who love our Lord Jesus Christ with undying love" (Eph. 6:24, F. F. Bruce trans.).

"others Needs over mine."

— Love one another, As Christ —
Matthew.

Babylon as whore has
many harlots.
Sobanus ot truth

Resources for Developing Loving Families

Oops! I Forgot My Wife
by Doyle Roth

We often think of marriage problems in terms of in-laws, finances, fidelity, or personality clashes. But these issues trace back to a simpler source. It's called self-centeredness and few men leave it behind at the altar.

That's why this marriage book takes the form of a story. Told through an exchange of emails, it follows the adventures and misfortunes of a guy who is so bad at husbanding he wakes up one morning on the brink of divorce. Only then does he learn what it really means to "love your wife as Christ loves the church." It tells the story of one marriage, flaws and all. It's not pretty or sanitized, but any husband or wife willing to examine their heart will see the truth in the story and benefit from it. There's also another reason to take a look. *Oops!* was written by a church elder who has been successfully counseling couples for over thirty years using the truth of Scripture and the love of Christ.

The story presented in this book serves as a great example of how godly supporters in local churches can use biblical wisdom to bless troubled couples. An ideal book for any couple that could use a few pointers but doesn't like to study.

"Most of us men could use help with our marriages, but most of us have little patience for touchy-feely, psycho-babbly marriage books written in professional counseling language. Bravo to Doyle Roth, who in *Oops!* addresses us sorry husbands using his own cowboy wisdom and wit -- loaded with ammunition to demolish male self-centeredness, yet still raw enough to engage the typical American male."

-- Douglas Hsu, Executive Editor, Advancing Native Missions

"This book is great and as refreshing an approach as its title! ...I have read many books about communication skills, etc., and biblical counseling, and this is by far the best book I have personally ever read on biblical counseling concerning relationships between men and women. ...this book touches the heart and is such an easy read."

-- Dawna Litz, Lighting the Way Worldwide

Lewis & Roth Publishers ◆ *800.477.3239*
Download sample chapters at www.lewisandroth.org

RESOURCES FOR DEVELOPING LOVING FAMILIES

Oops! We Forgot the Kids
by Doyle Roth

Thousands of couples have read Doyle Roth's *Oops! I Forgot My Wife*. Now the subject is parenting. Once again, you'll think he's sneaking a peak at your family! Doyle's strategy is much the same: combine situations from his decades in family counseling into one engaging story, have the characters involved discuss effective parenting principles via email, add the "how tos" and season it all with humor and solid counsel from the Scriptures.

Oops! We Forgot the Kids teaches achievable parenting skills to everyday dads and moms who want to be effective down in the trenches of parenting. Real life problems and questions, some old-fashioned horse sense and time-tested biblical insight combine to give parents hope and help.

Filled with down-to-earth advice, good humor and biblical insights from decades of family intervention, is sure to bring you a deeper appreciation of your own family—and some hints on making it even better. (Not perfect, just better.)

Oops! I Forgot My Wife Audio Book
by Doyle Roth

Professional actors breathe life into Doyle Roth's art-imitating-life tale of marriage, self-centerednes and commitment.

This audio book is an abridged version of the original text. 4 Audio CDs; 4 hours; 49 minutes

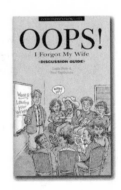

Oops! I Forgot My Wife Discussion Guide
by Doyle Roth

The *Oops! I Forgot My Wife Discussion Guide* combines helpful and humorous insights from the book, along with practical questions to fuel hearty discussion. Some of the questions will prompt you to assess how things stand in your marriage, while others will inspire you to invest creatively in your best friendship.

Lewis & Roth Publishers ◆ *800.477.3239*
Download sample chapters at www.lewisandroth.org

Resources for Developing Loving Christian Community & Leadership

Leading With Love
Leading With Love Study Guide
by Alexander Strauch

Though a wealth of good material is available on the leadership qualities of courage, charisma, discipline, vision and decisiveness, few books for church leaders include anything about love. This is a major oversight since the New Testament is clear that love is indispensable to service. *Leading with Love* is written for leaders and teachers at every level of leadership within the local church.

"This message is urgently needed by all of us. You may have many talents and spiritual gifts, but without the love that this book speaks about, you don't really have much at all."

— *George Verwer, Founder & President, Operation Mobilization*

"*Leading with Love* is a superb exposition of how the followers of Incarnate Love should live out their love. I found it deeply challenging as, in simple, direct language, with apt quotes and illustrations, it probed one and another area of heart, soul and relationships with the insistent demand of the second of the greatest commandments."

— *Robert Gordon, Faculty, University of Cambridge*

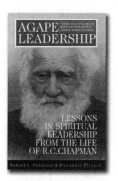

Agape Leadership
by Robert L. Peterson & Alexander Strauch

One of our greatest need as we develop loving church community is the need for role models. Though largely unknown today, Robert Chapman (1803-1902) serves as just such an example. Featuring twelve lessons drawn from Chapman's life, *Agape Leadership* demonstrates godly, loving, pastoral leadership in action.

"It will challenge you to be a better leader, a more committed believer, and a brighter light to the world."

— *Greg Stephenson, Grace Ministries International*

"R.C. Chapman's life is a vivid illustration of Jesus' teaching. I have given a copy of the book to pastors and ministry leaders with the prayer that we might reject a professional ministry mindset and follow Jesus as Chapman did."

— *Peter Hubbard, Pastor/Teacher,*
North Hills Community Church, Taylors, SC

Lewis & Roth Publishers ✦ *800.477.3239*
Download sample chapters at www.lewisandroth.org

RESOURCES FOR DEVELOPING LOVING CHRISTIAN COMMUNITY & LEADERSHIP

The Hospitality Commands
by Alexander Strauch

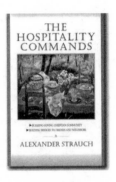

Hospitality may well be the best means we have to promote close, brotherly love in our church communities. Hospitality is also an effective tool for evangelism. The *Hospitality Commands* expounds every Scripture on the subject, explores all the biblical examples, lists the biblical fruits of Christian hospitality and makes practical suggestions. Also included are study questions and assignments for group discussion.

The New Testament Deacon: Minister of Mercy
The New Testament Deacon Study Guide
by Alexander Strauch

Deacons, as the New Testament teaches and as some of the sixteenth-century reformers discovered, are to be involved in a compassionate ministry of caring for the poor and needy. The deacons' ministry, therefore, is one that no church can afford to neglect. It is through the ministry of deacons that we make Christ's love a reality for many people A groundbreaking study of all of the biblical texts on the subject *The New Testament Deacon* will help you build a strong ministry in your church.

Love or Die: Christ's Wake-up Call to the Church
by Alexander Strauch

In his challenging exposition of Revelation 2:2-6, Strauch reminds us that a church can teach sound doctrine, be faithful to the gospel, be morally upright and hard working, and yet be lacking love and displeasing to Christ. Love can grow cold while outward religious performance appears acceptable--even praiseworthy. Part Two of the book is practical suggestions for stimulating love in the local church.

Study guide included, making this an exceptional tool for classes and small groups.

"But I have this against you, that you have abandoned the love you had at first."
— *Revelation 2:4*

Lewis & Roth Publishers ◆ *800.477.3239*
Download sample chapters at www.lewisandroth.org